This Book Belongs To

____

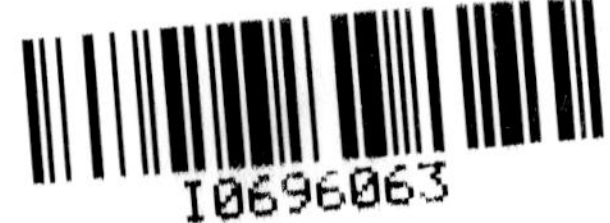

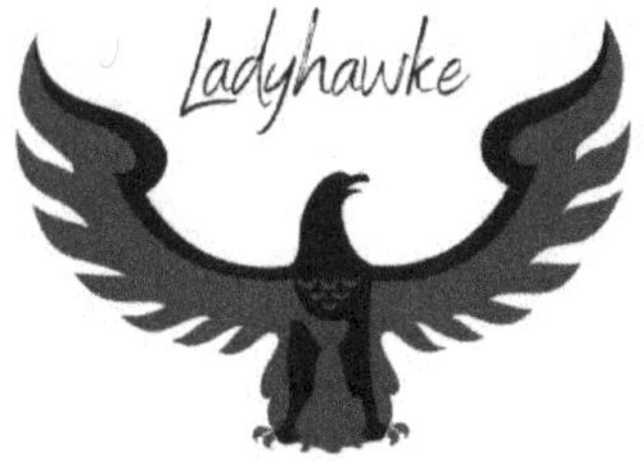

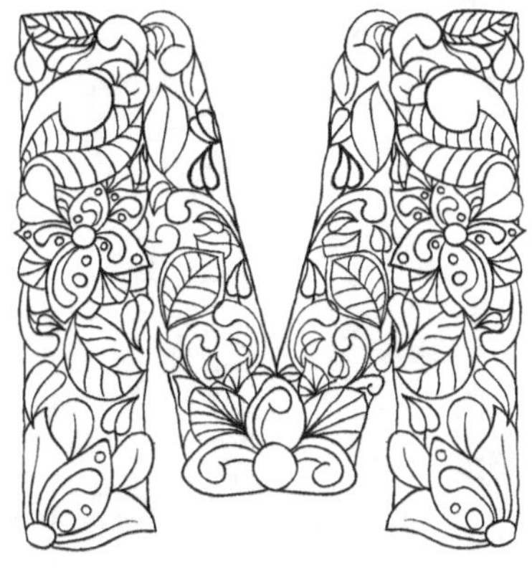andala

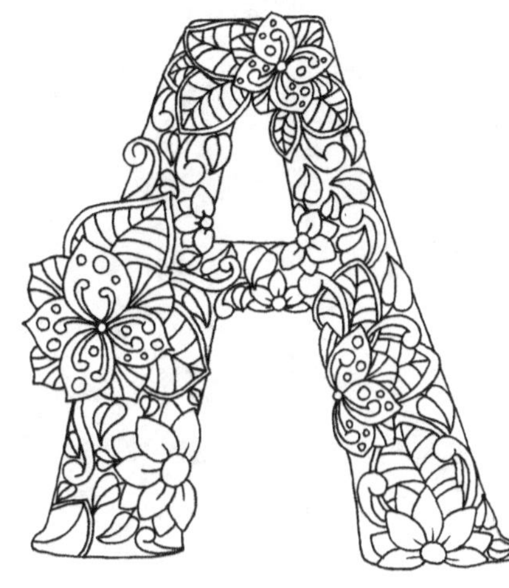lphabet

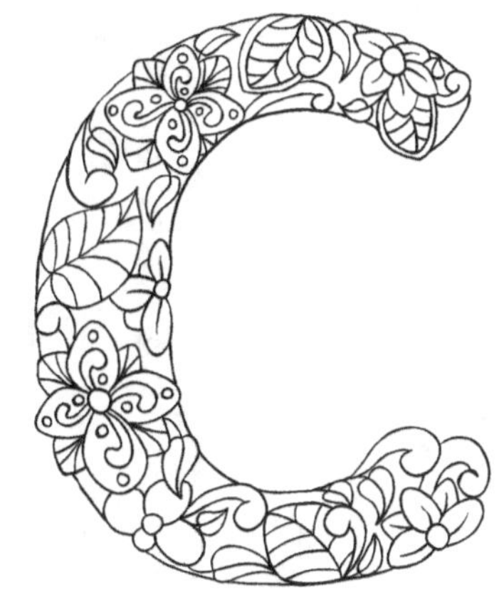oloring

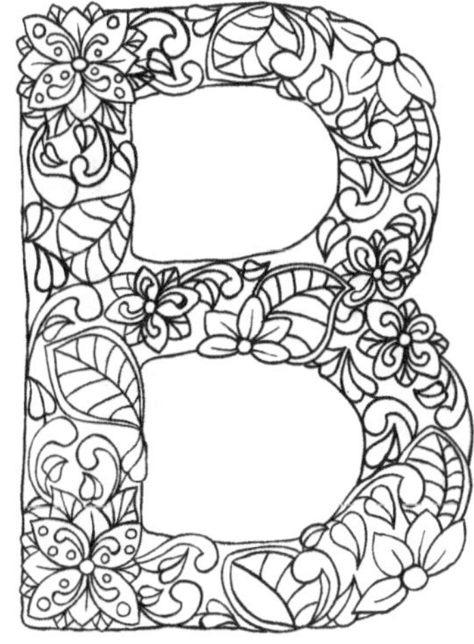ook

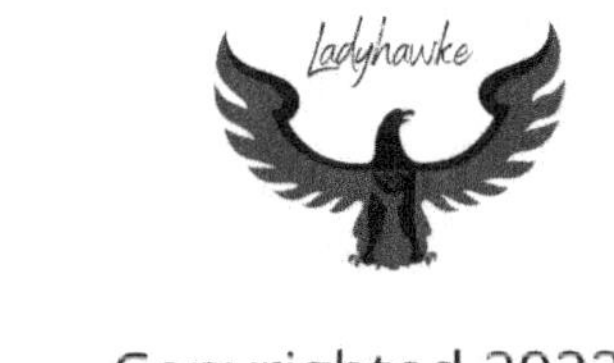

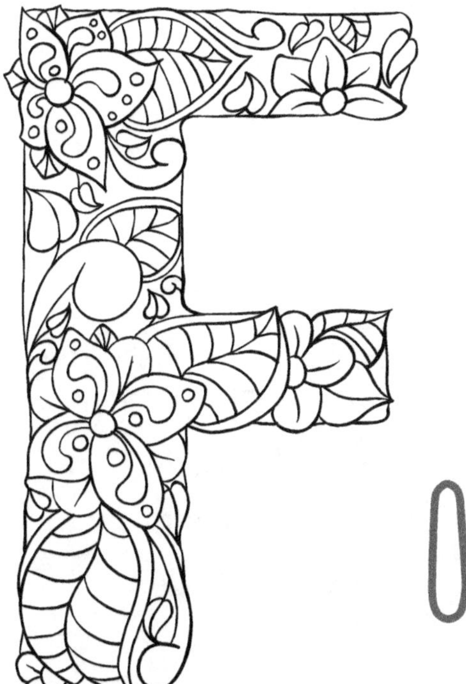

Flowered

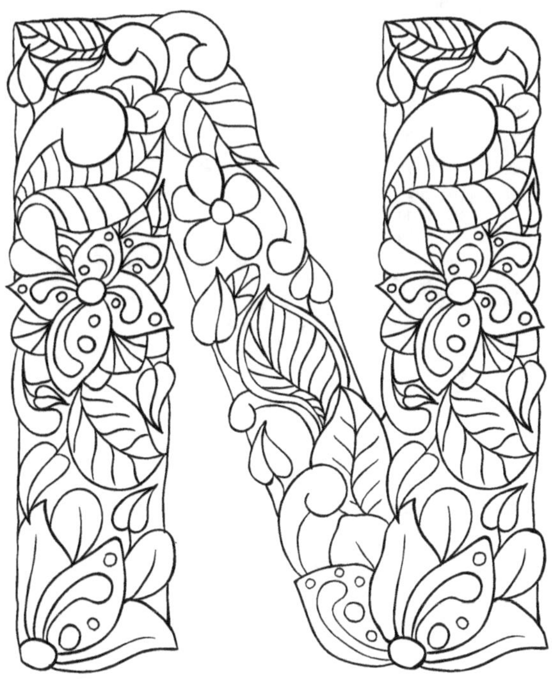

Numbers

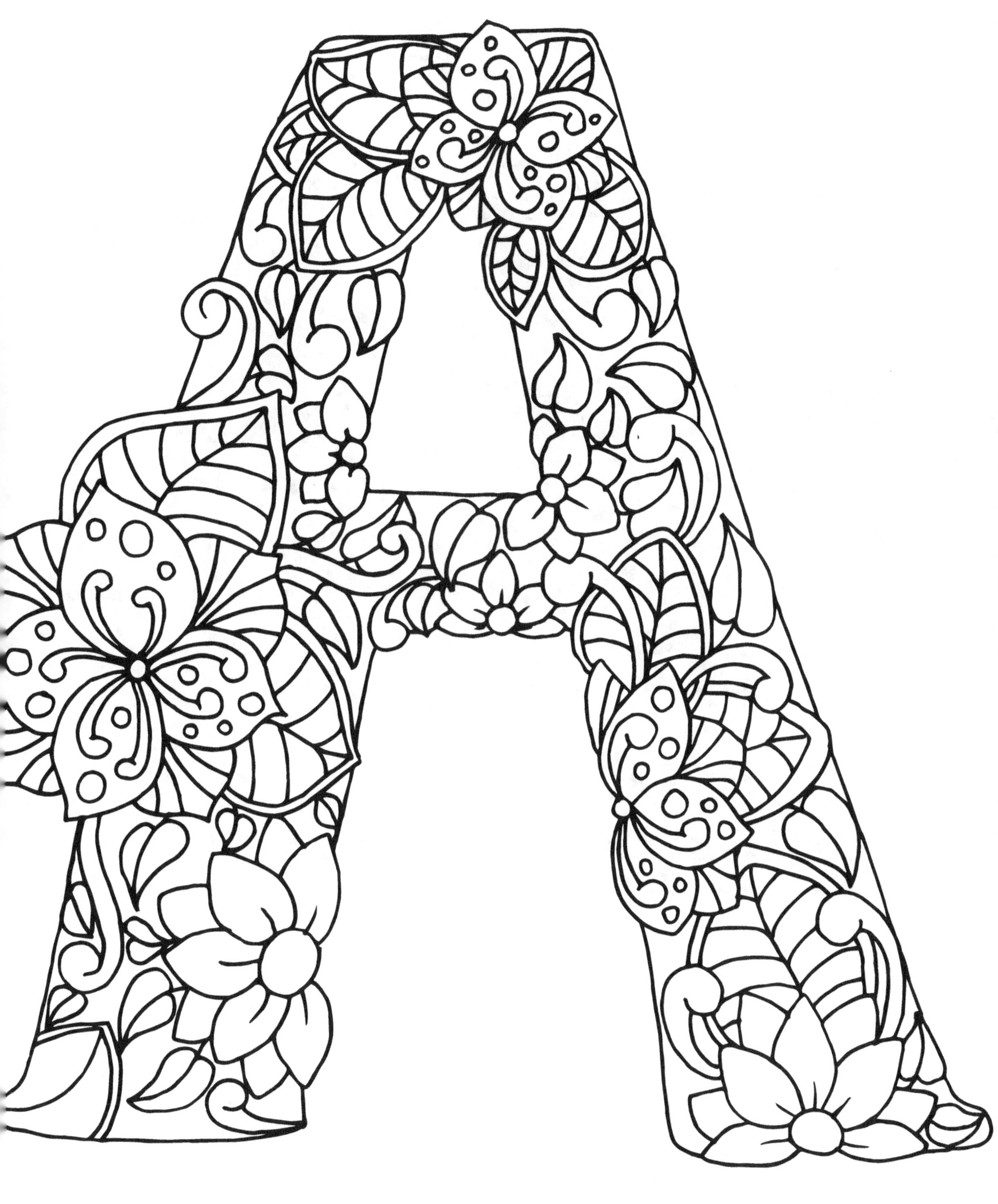

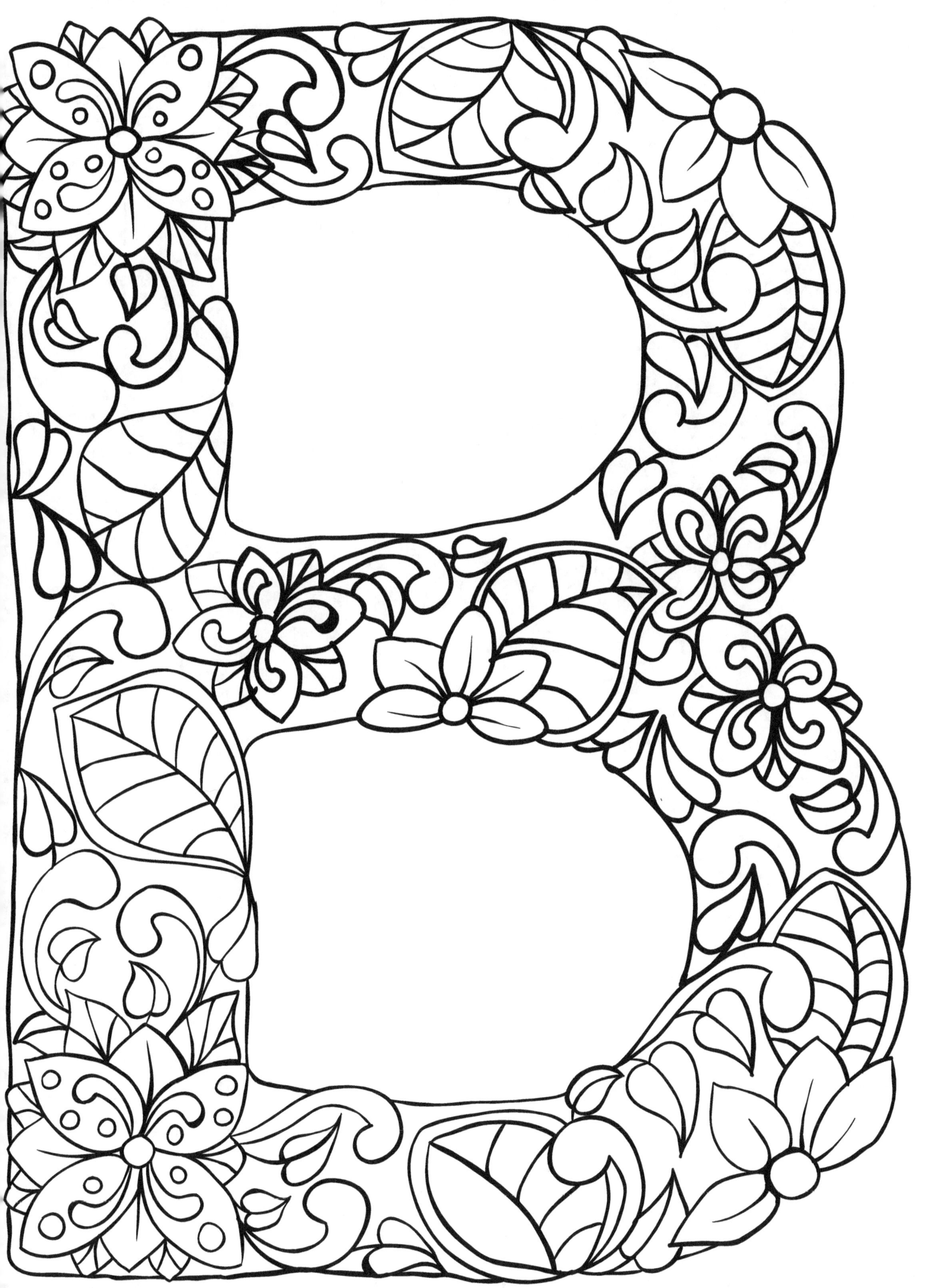

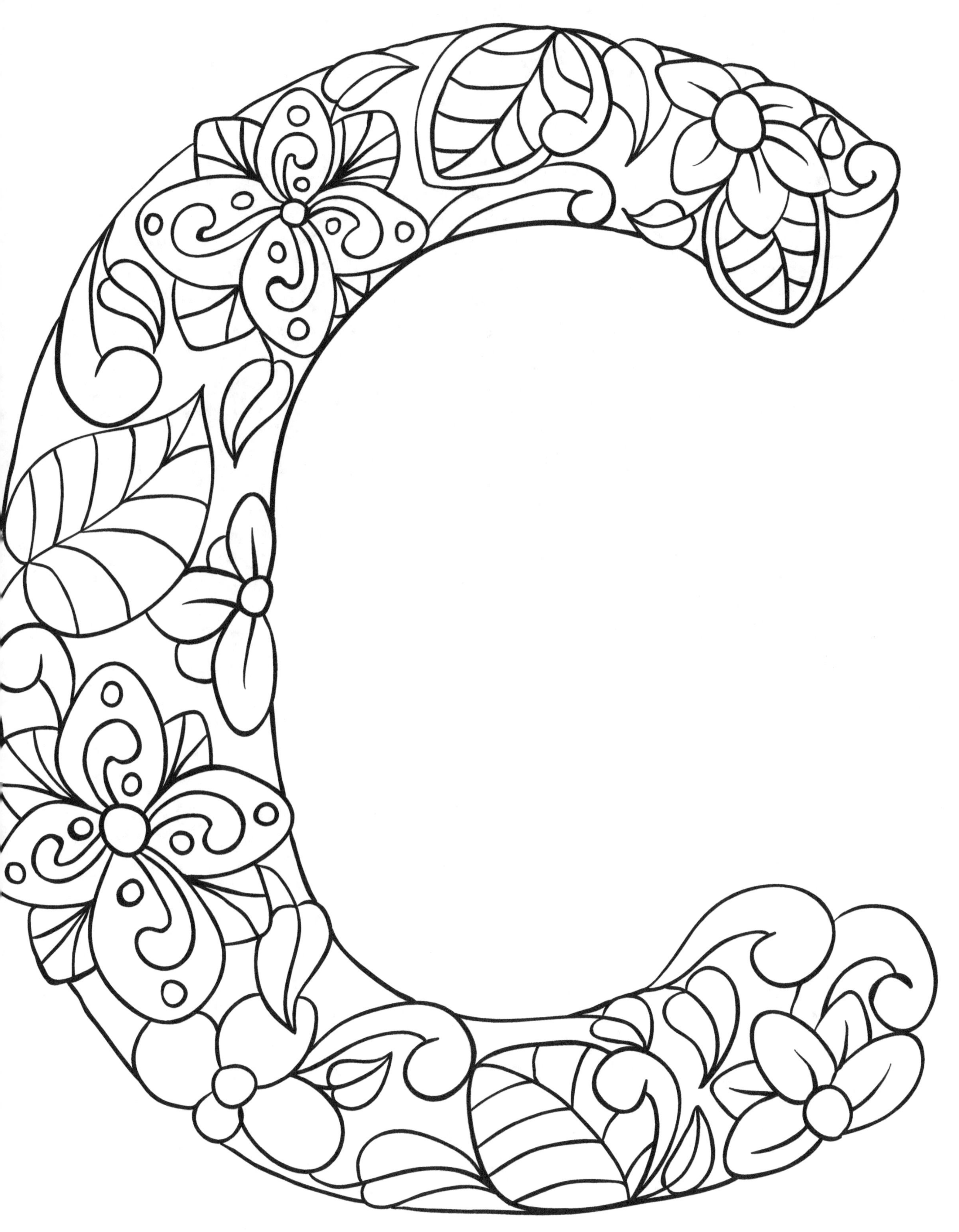

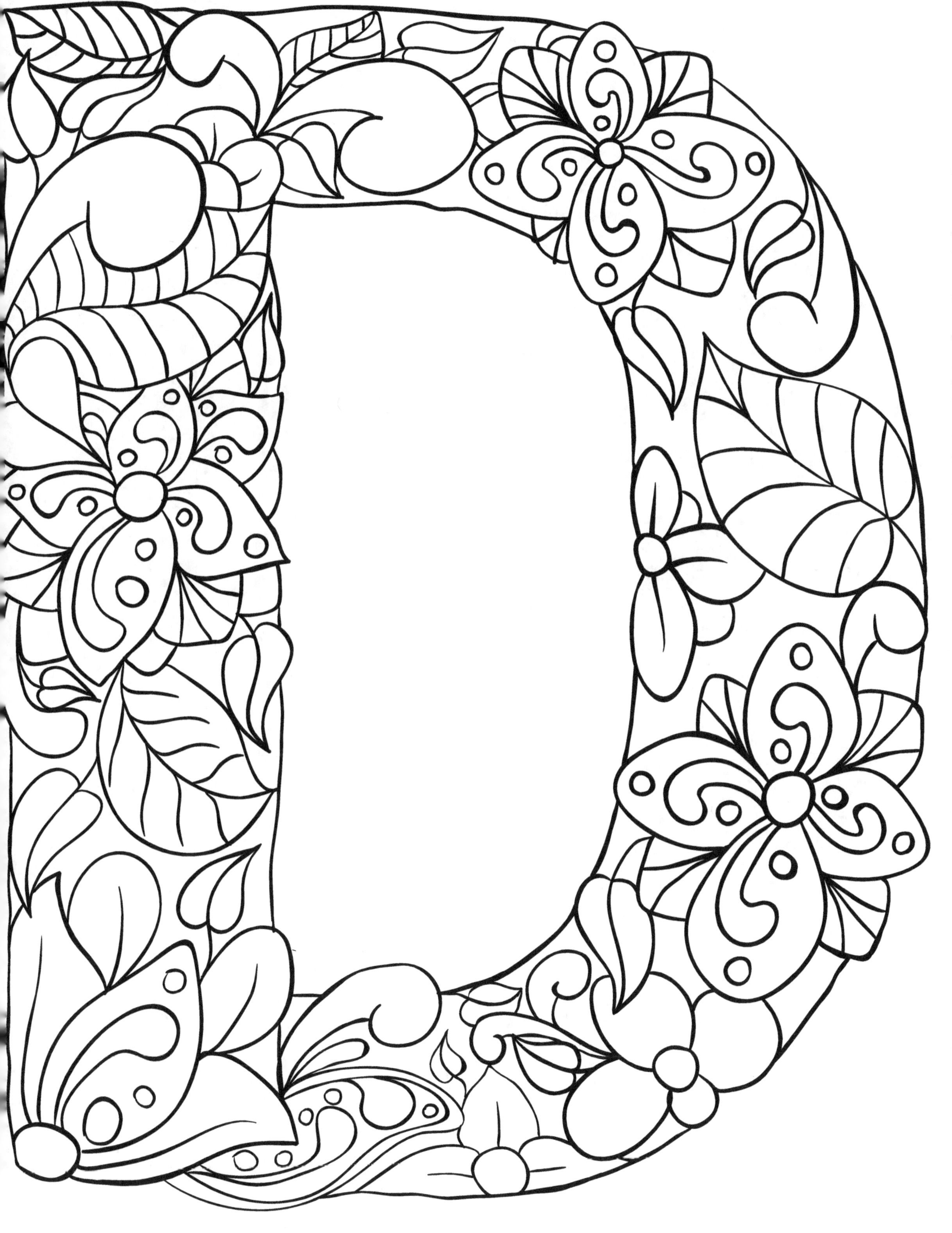

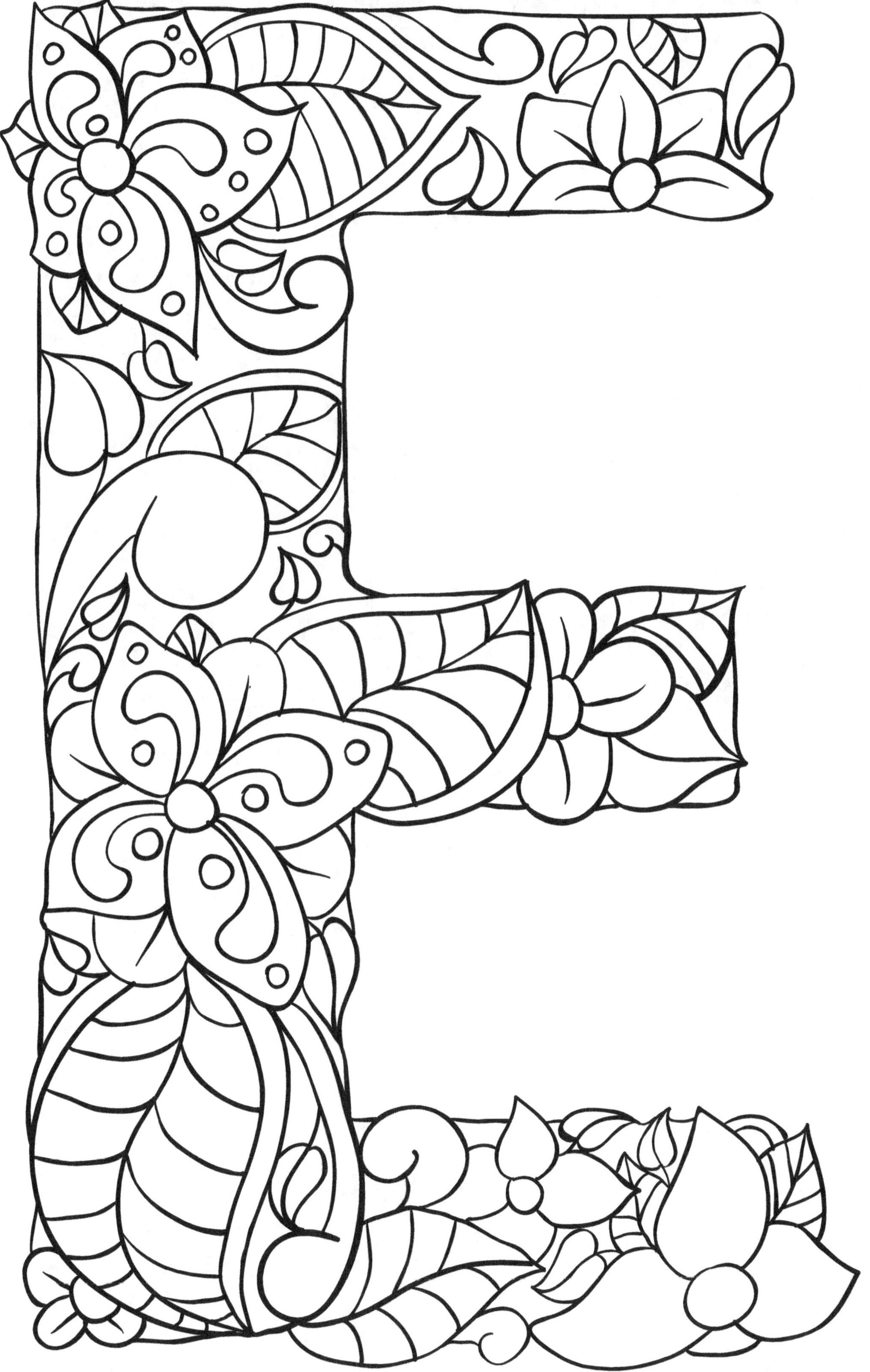

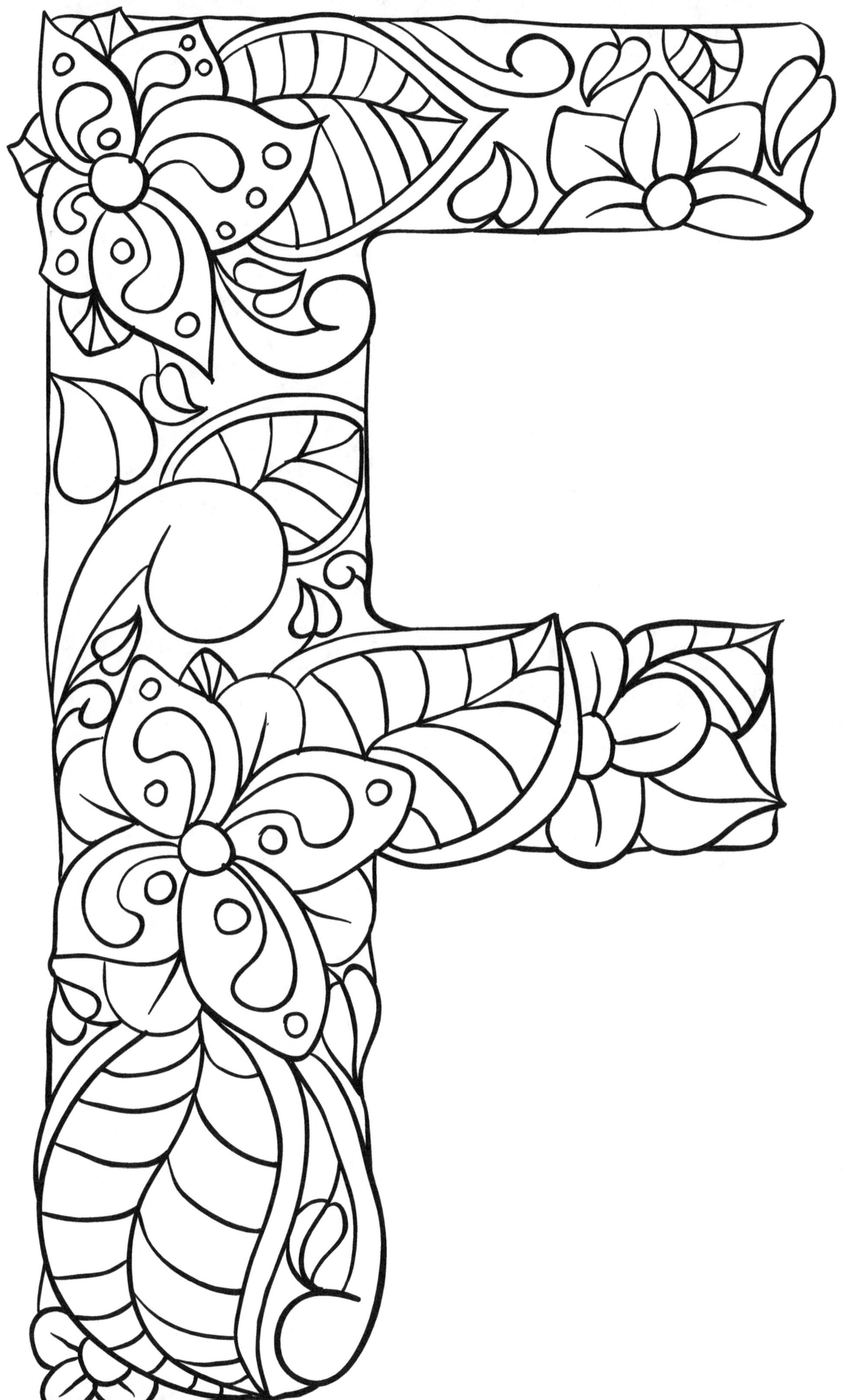

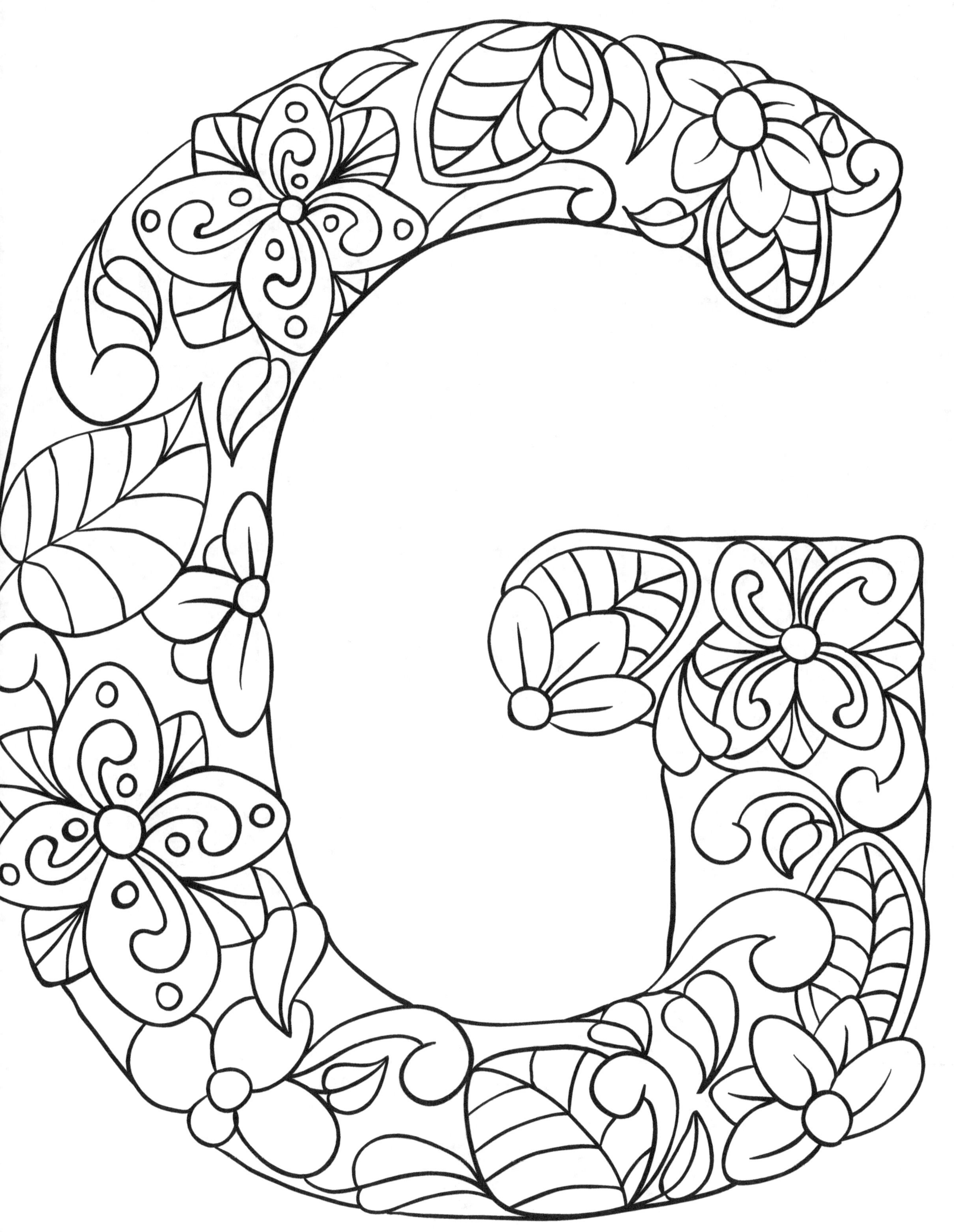

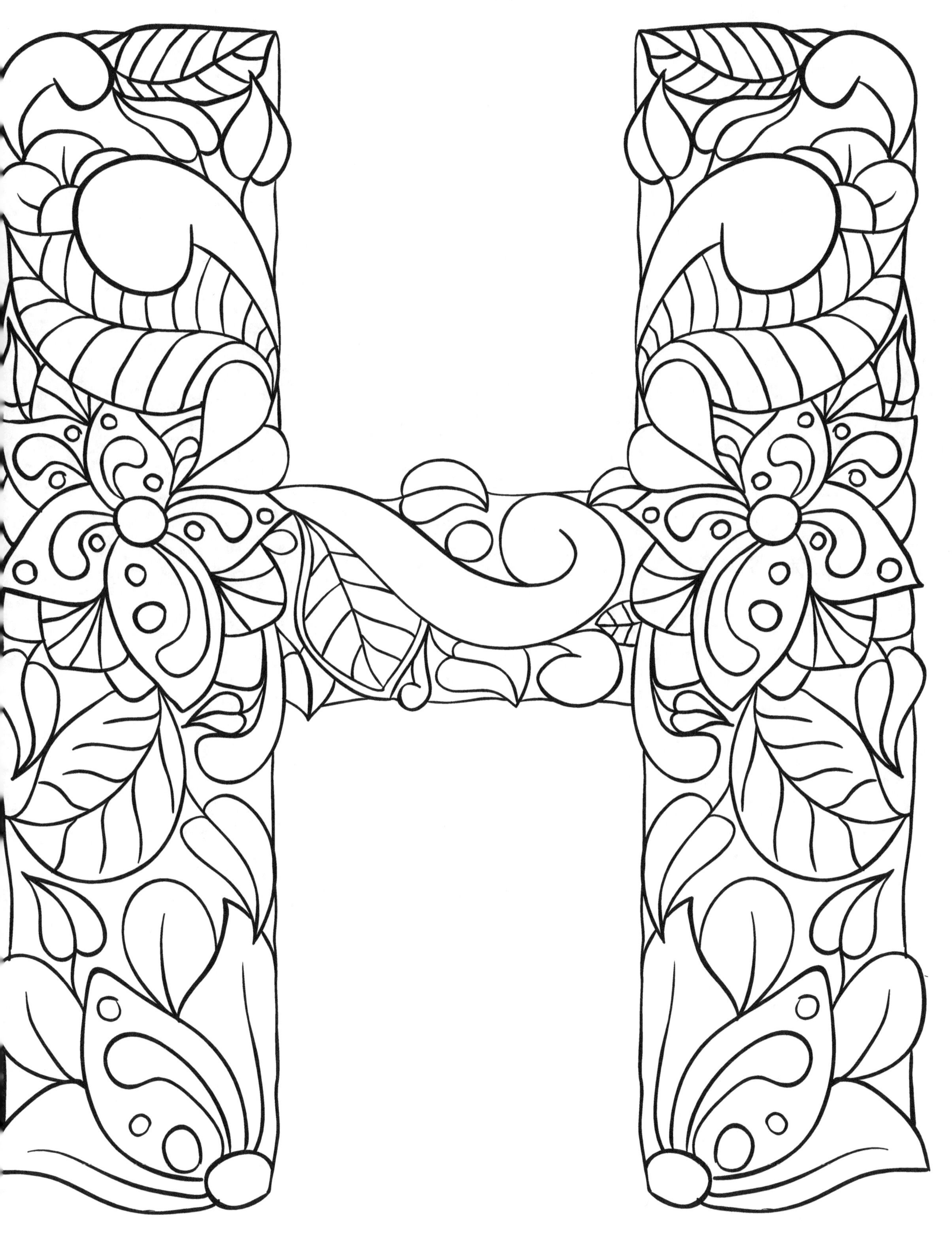

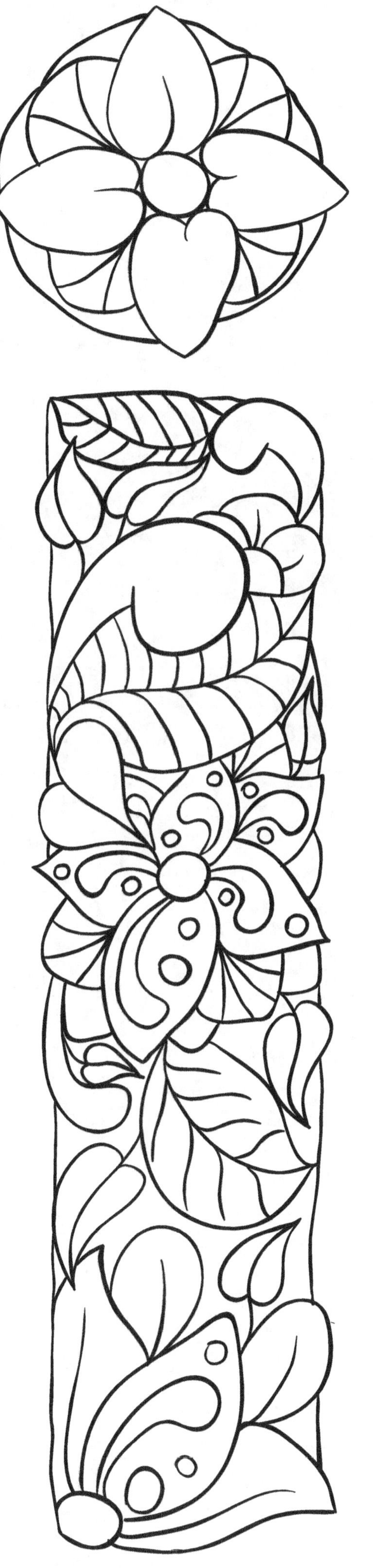

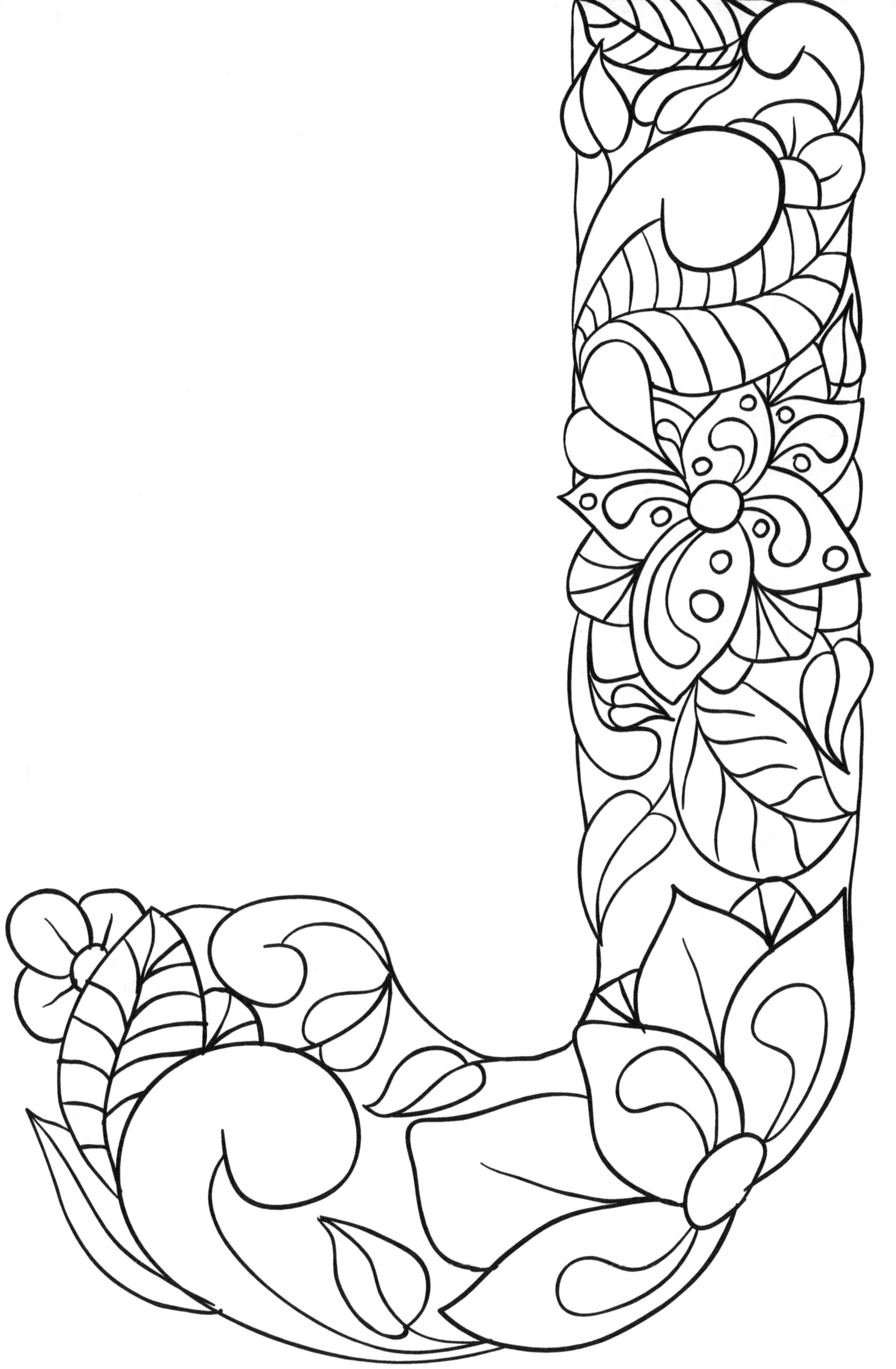

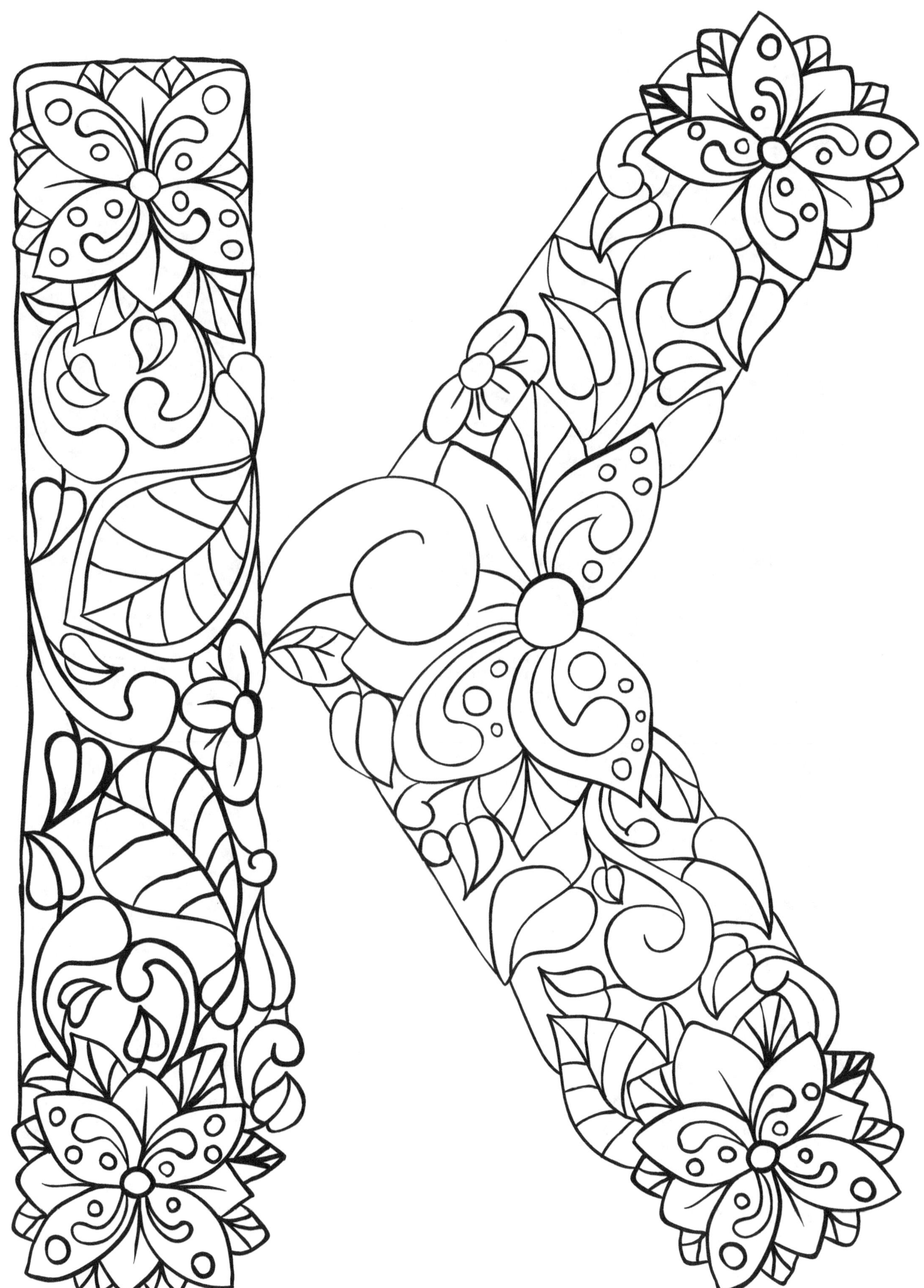

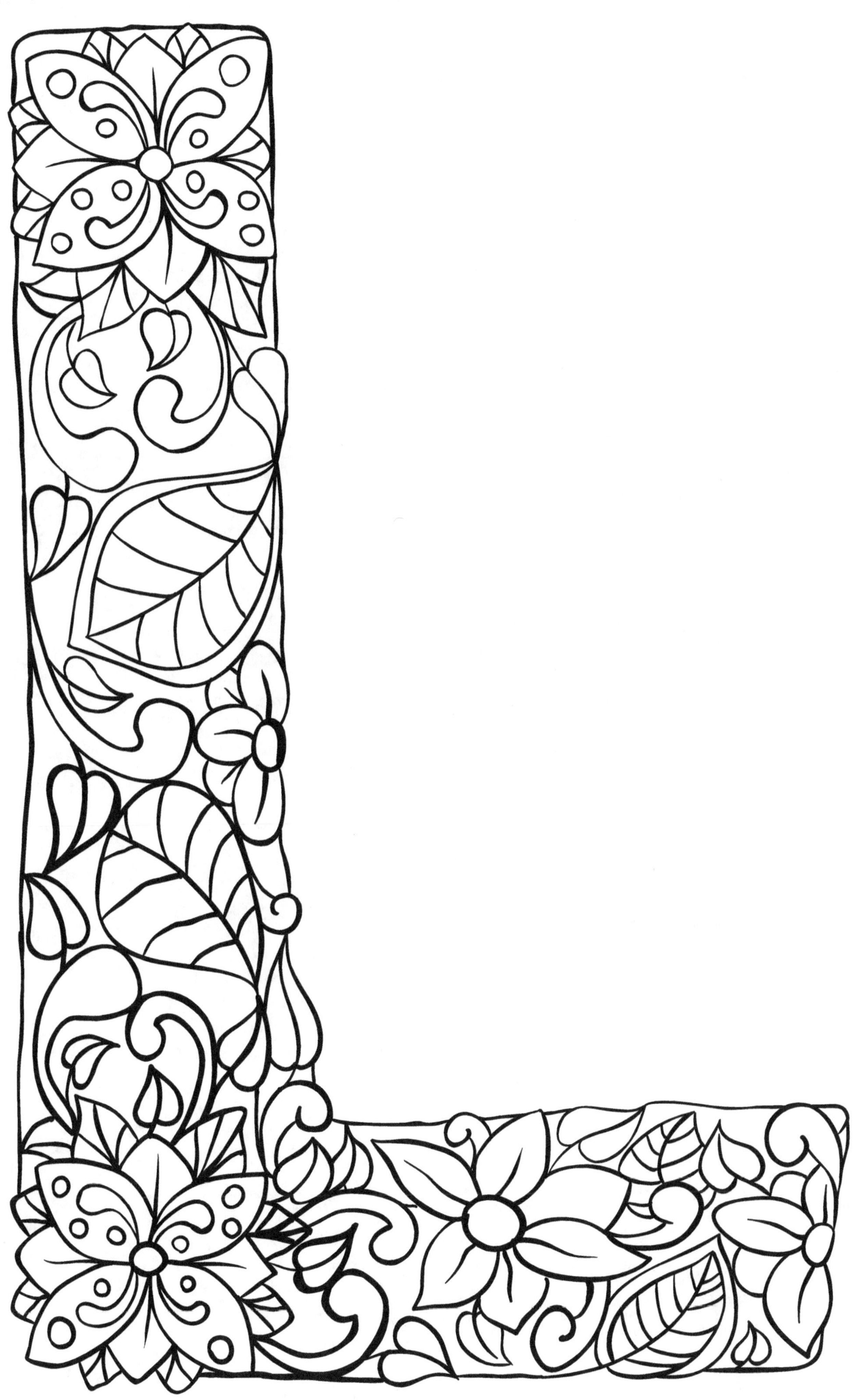

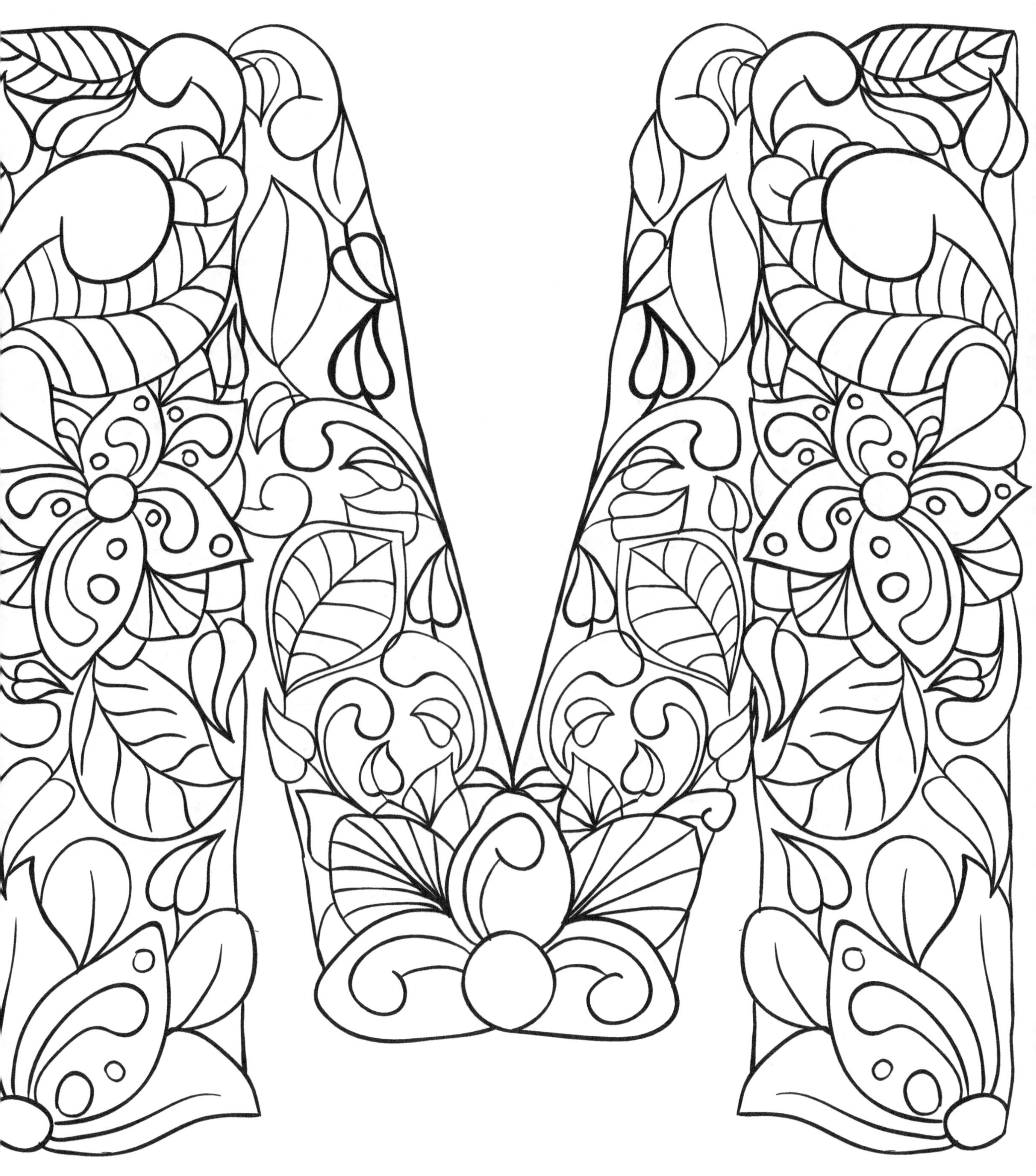

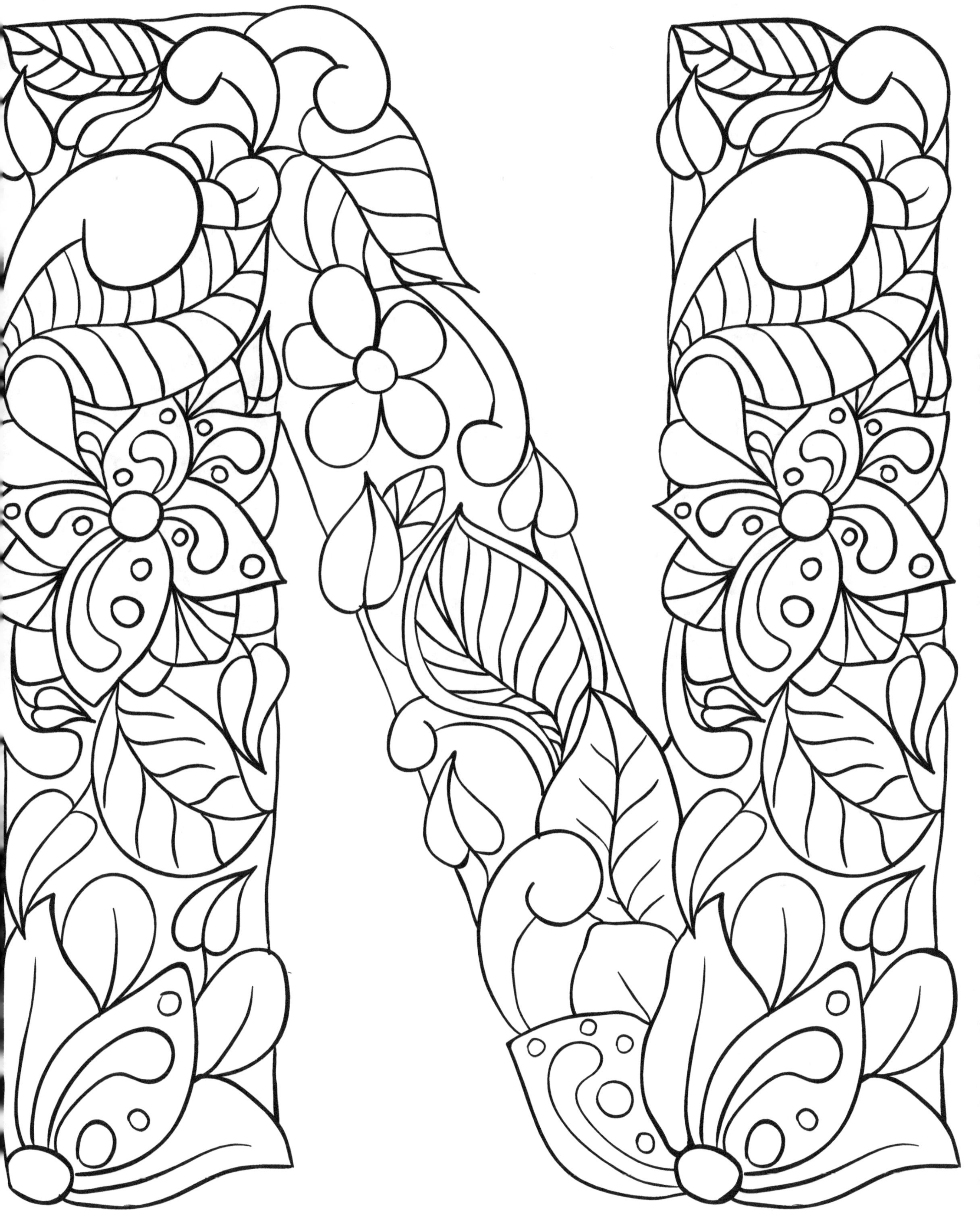

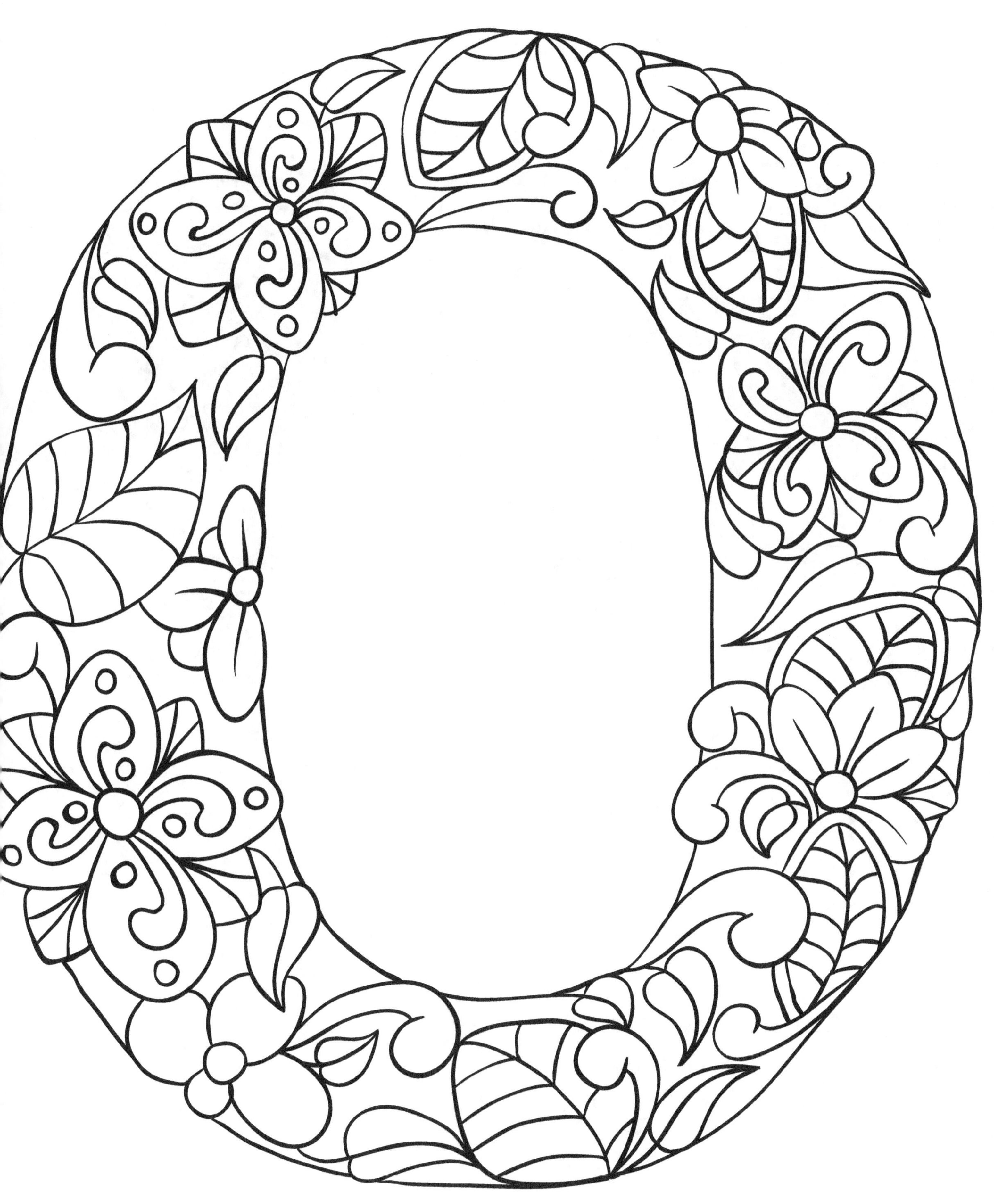

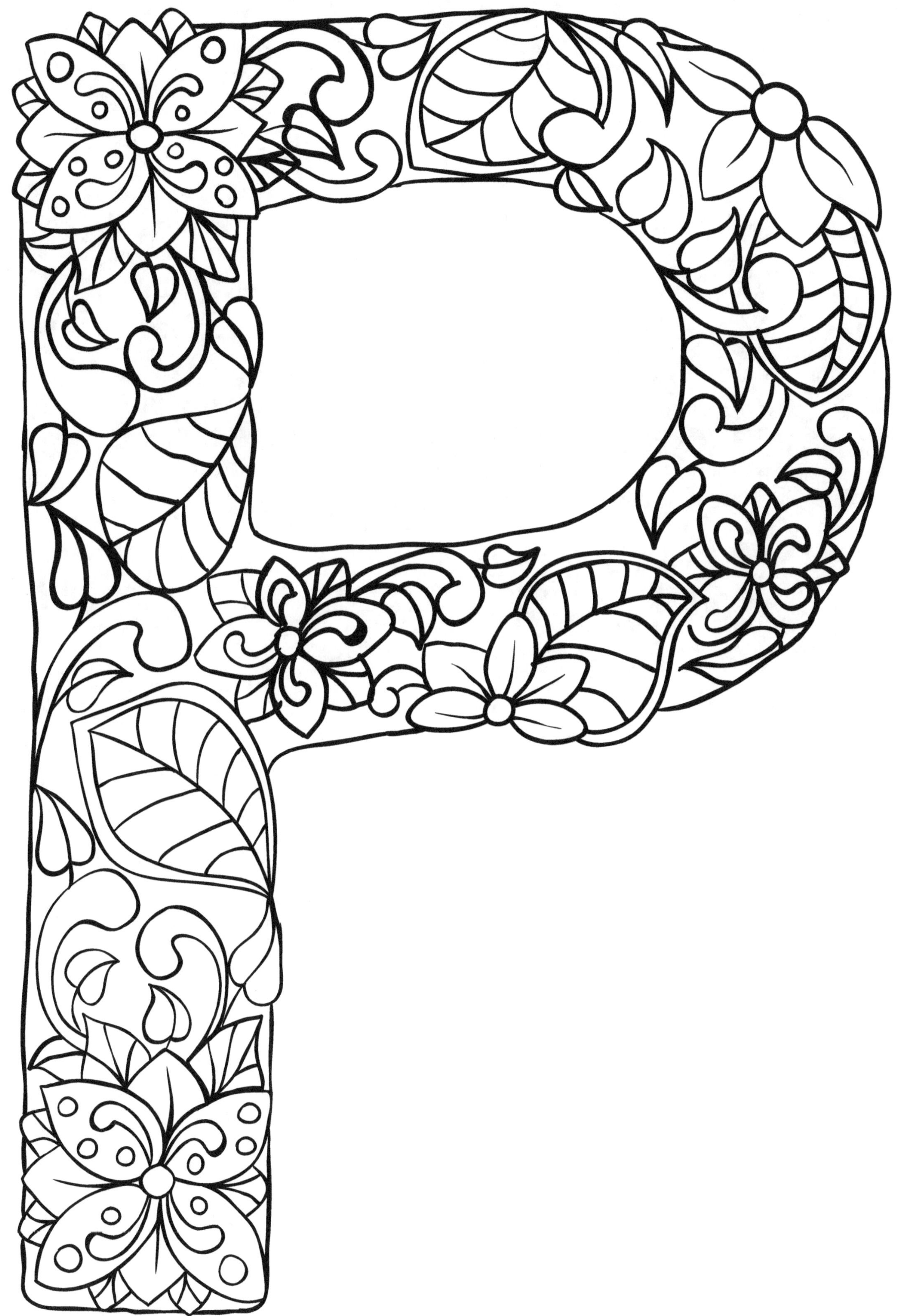

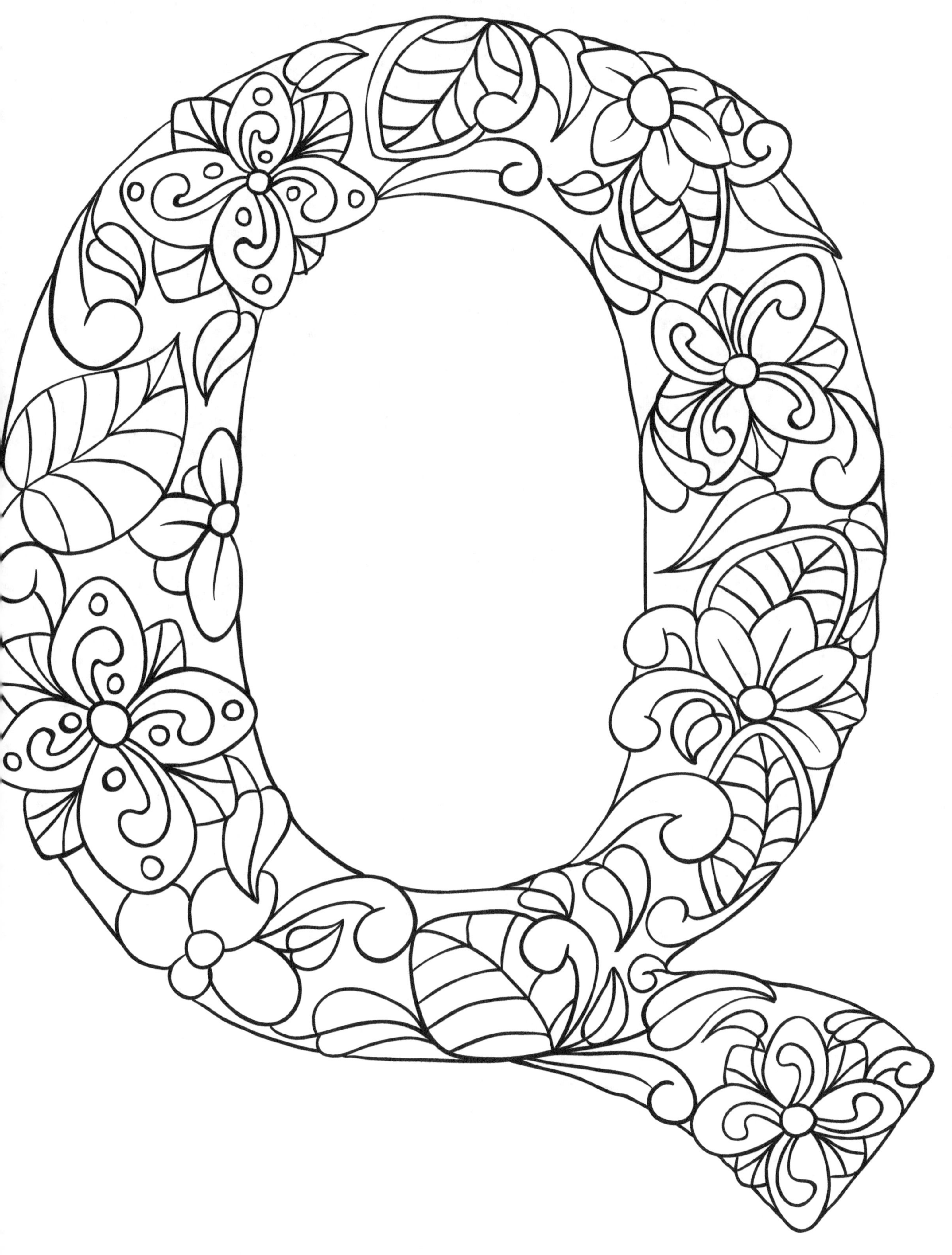

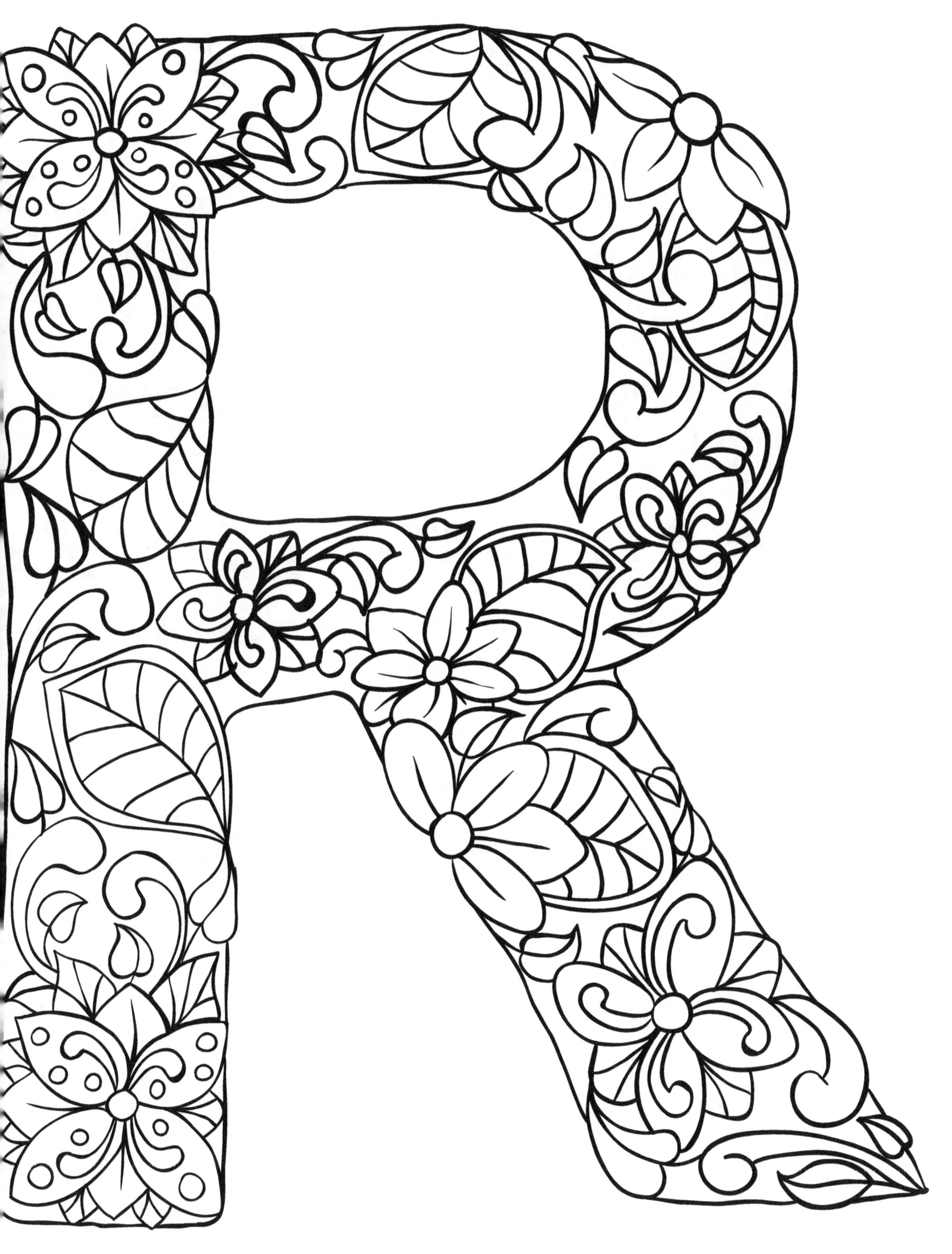

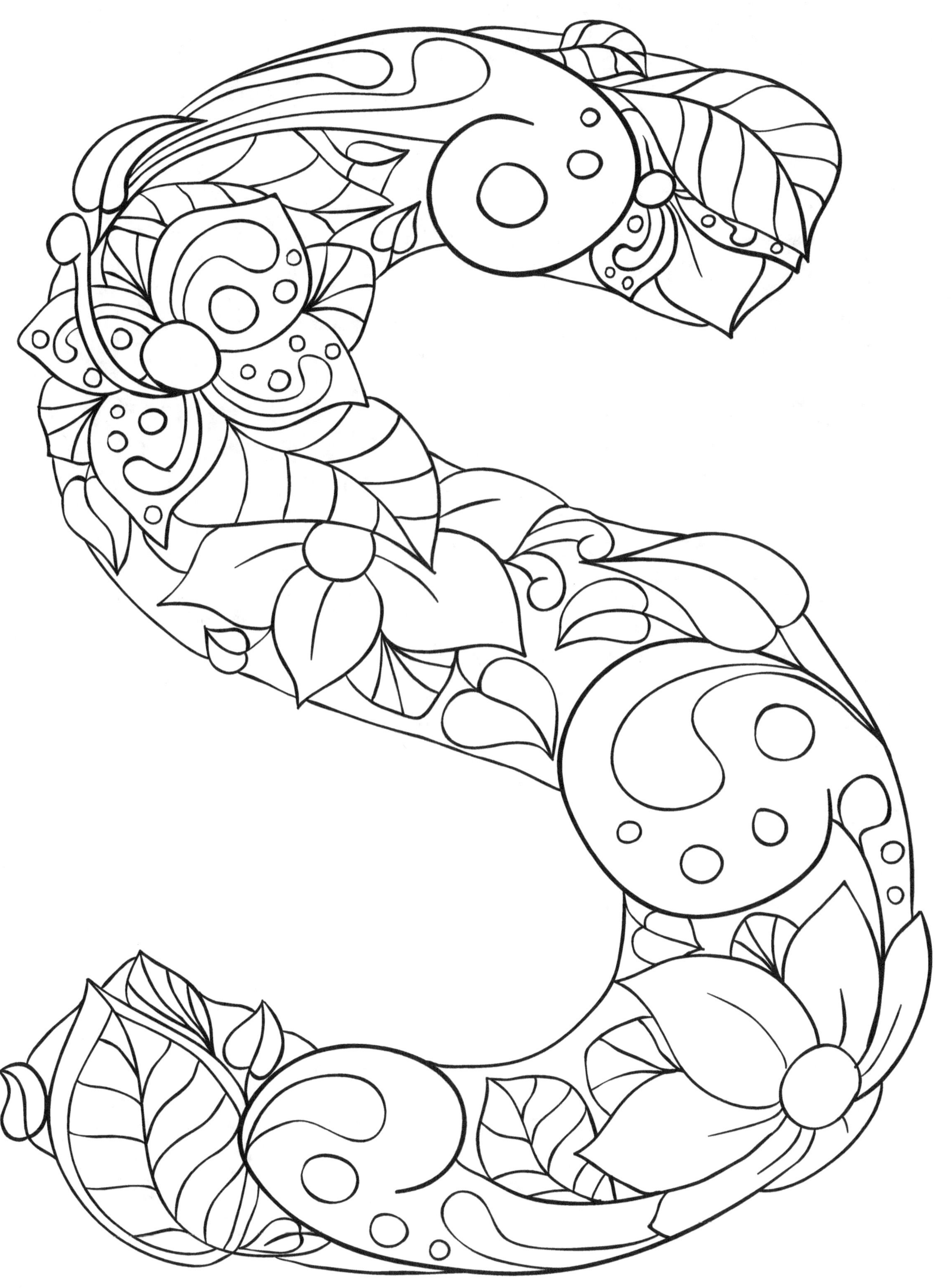

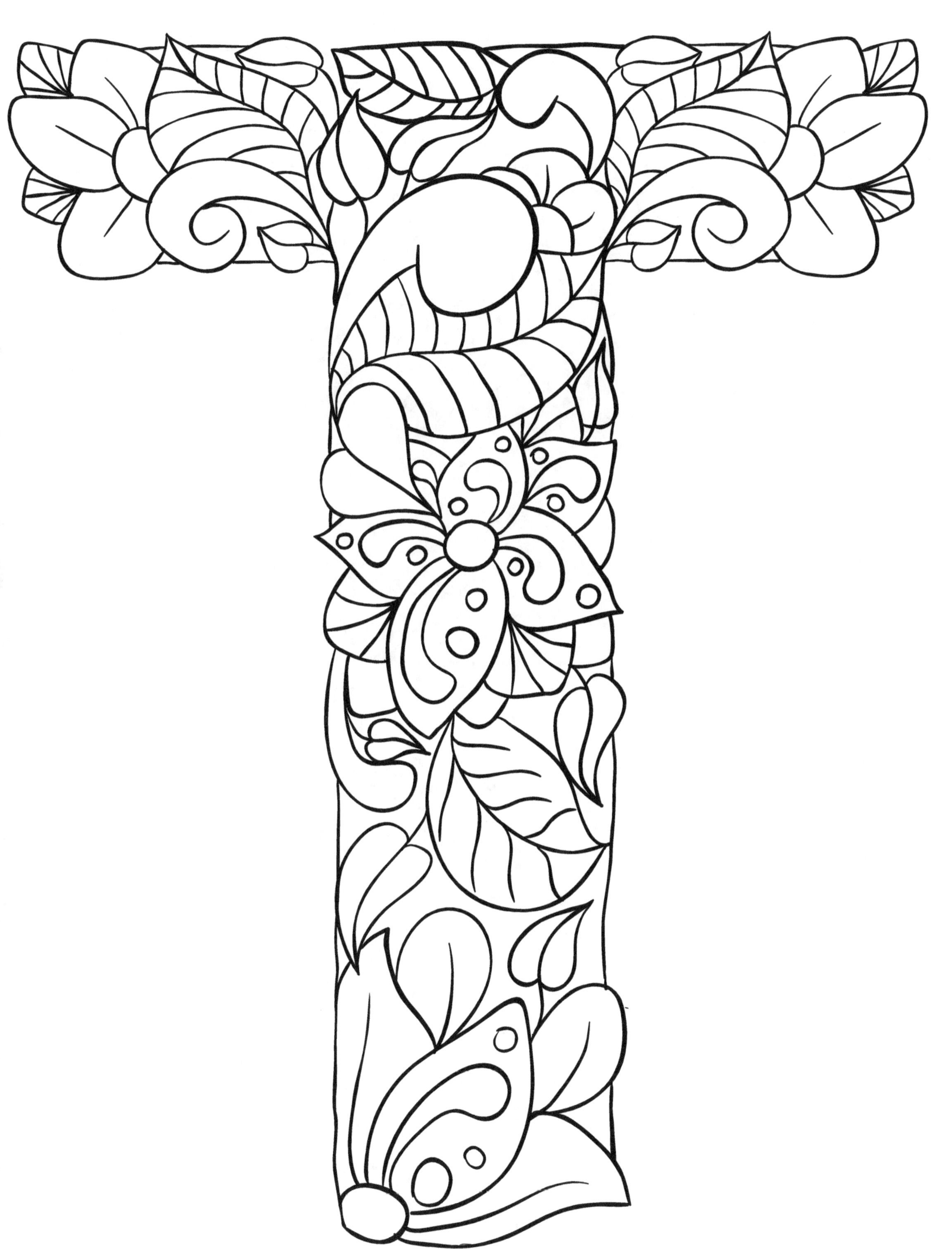

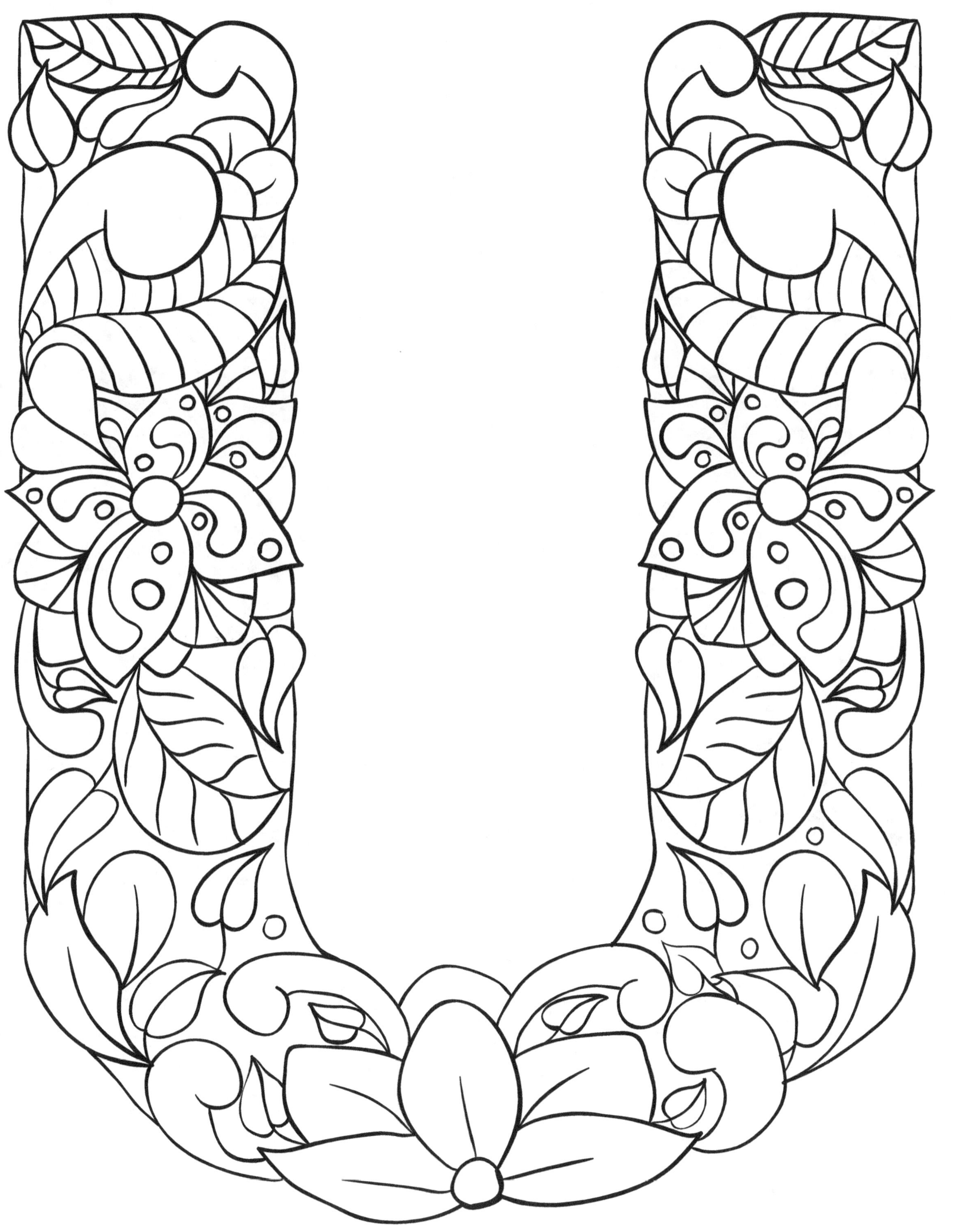

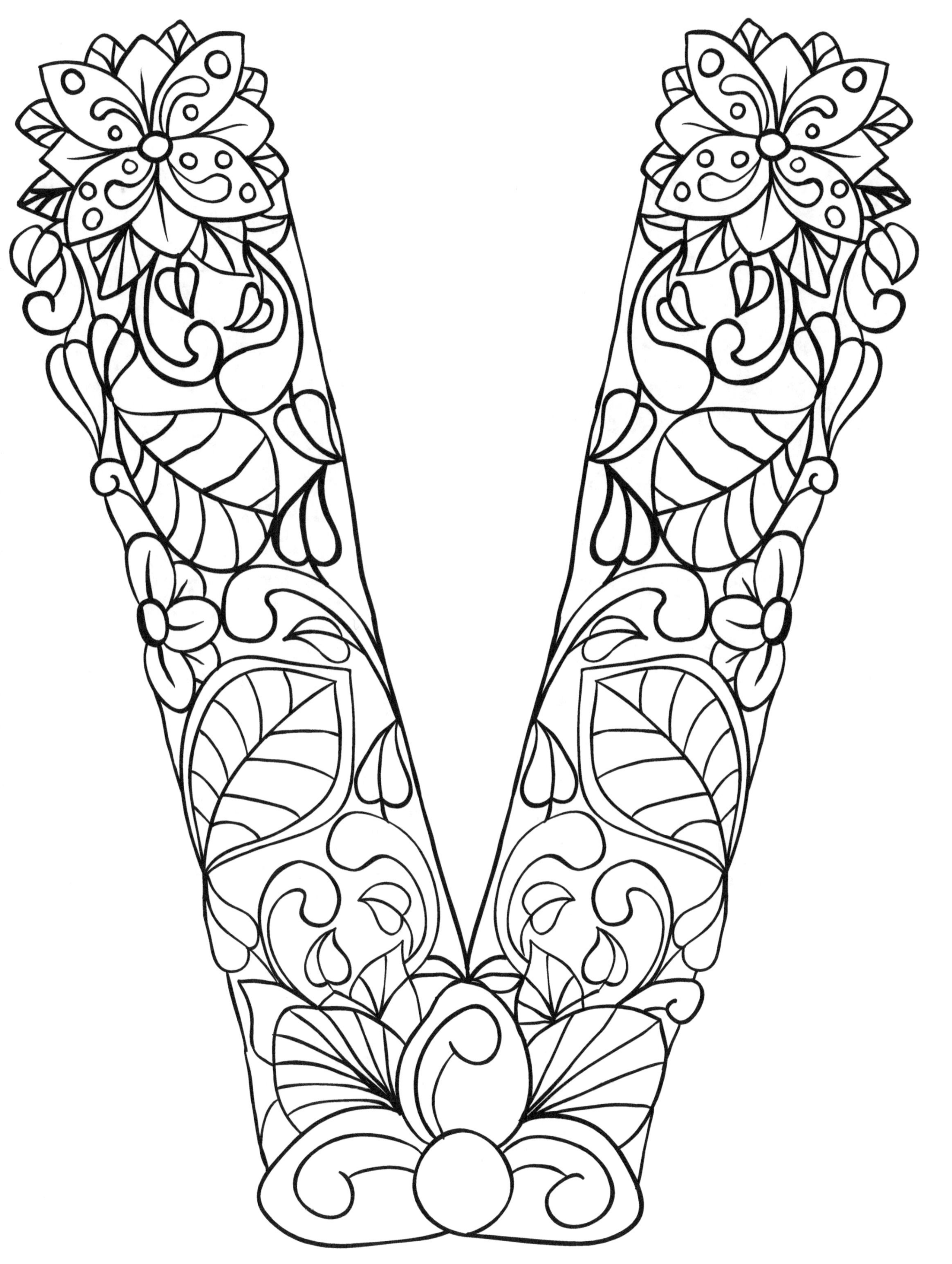

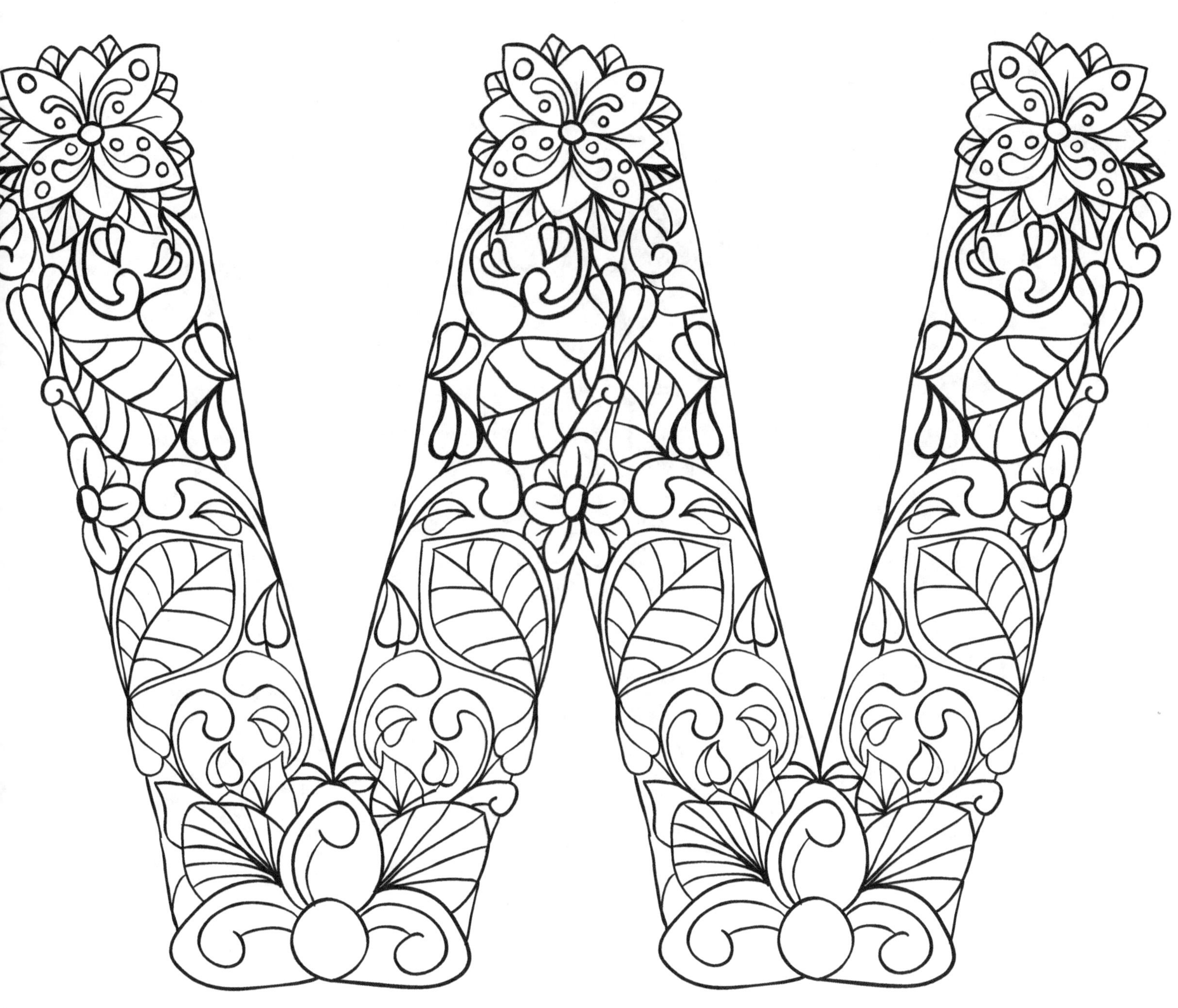

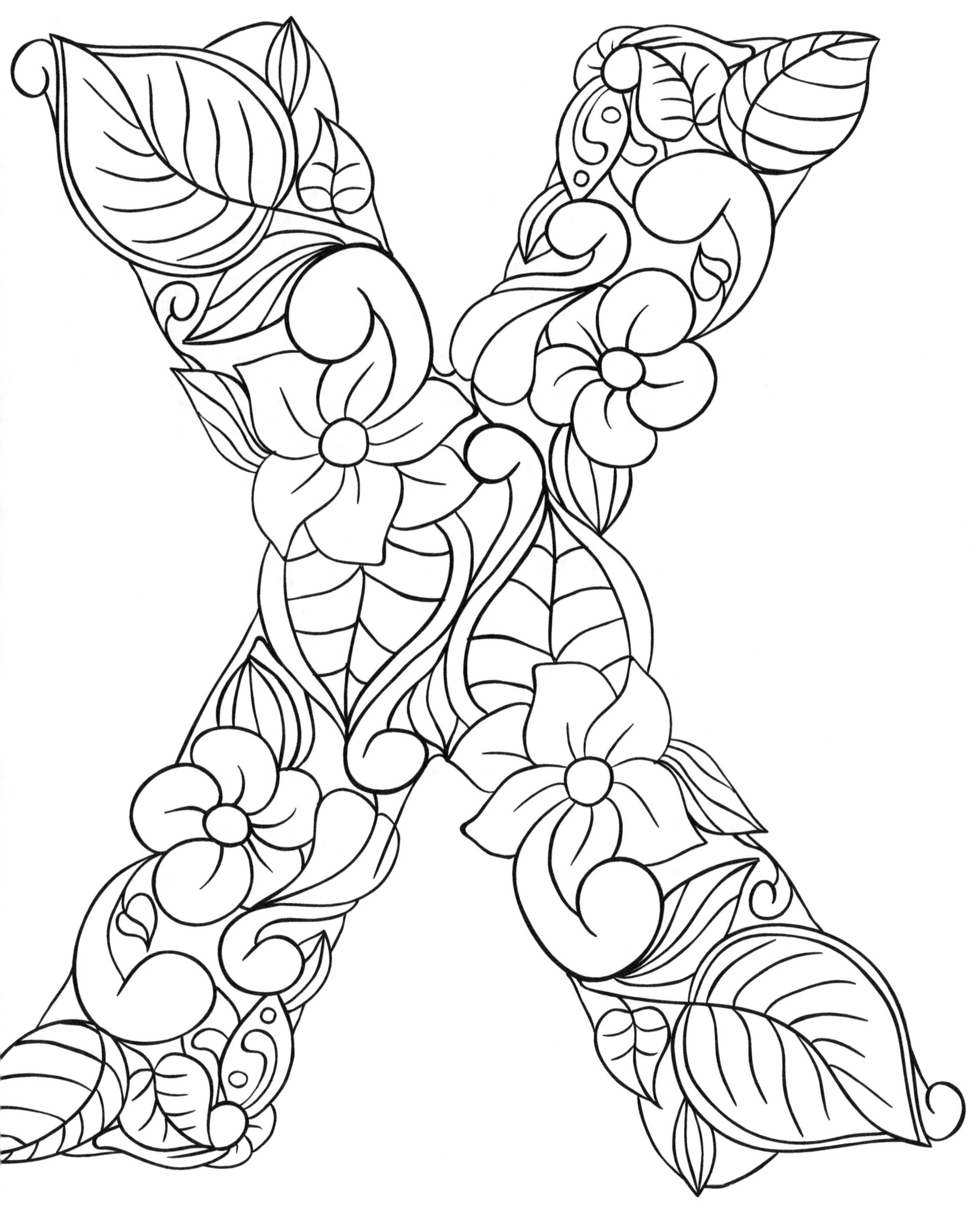

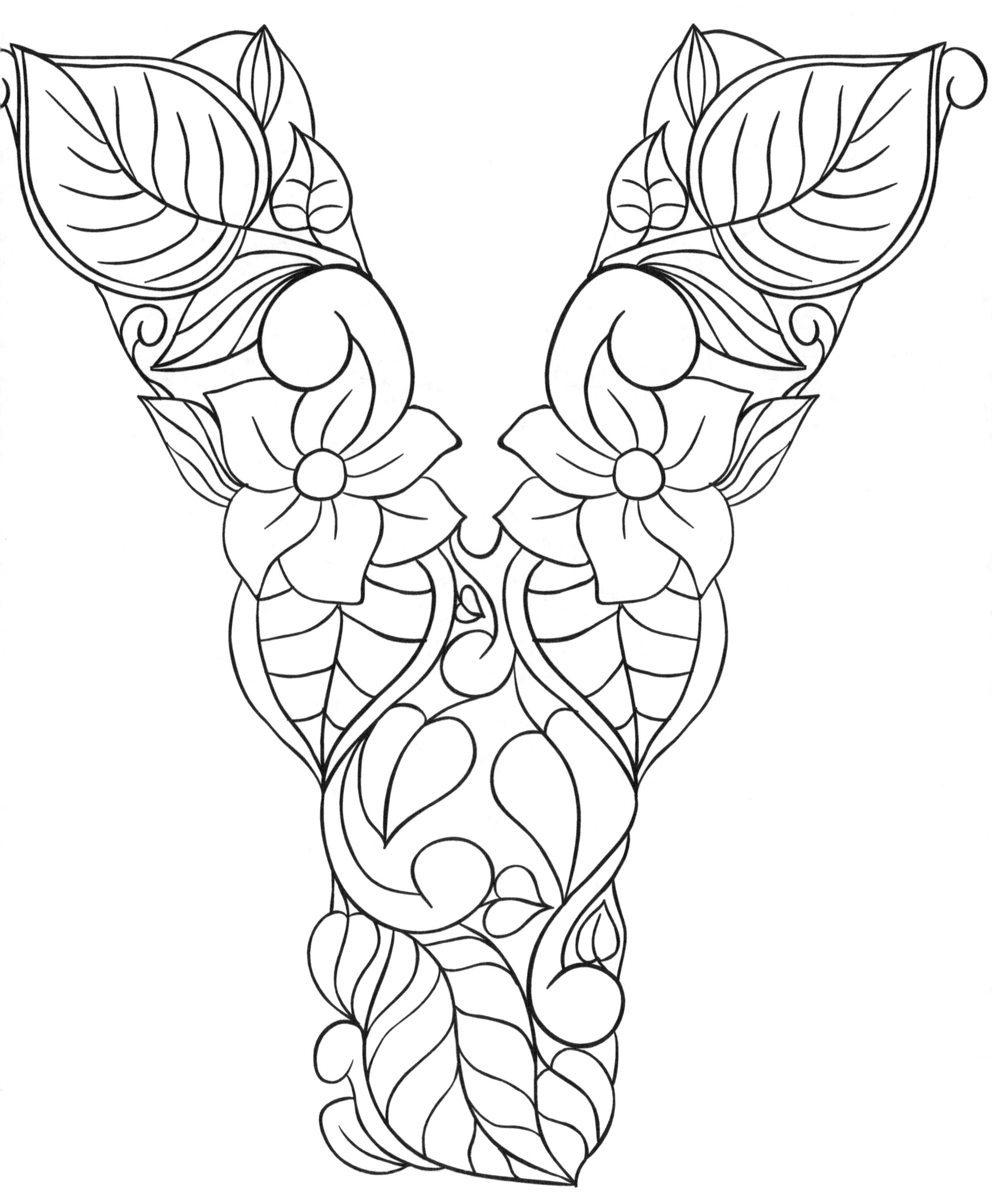

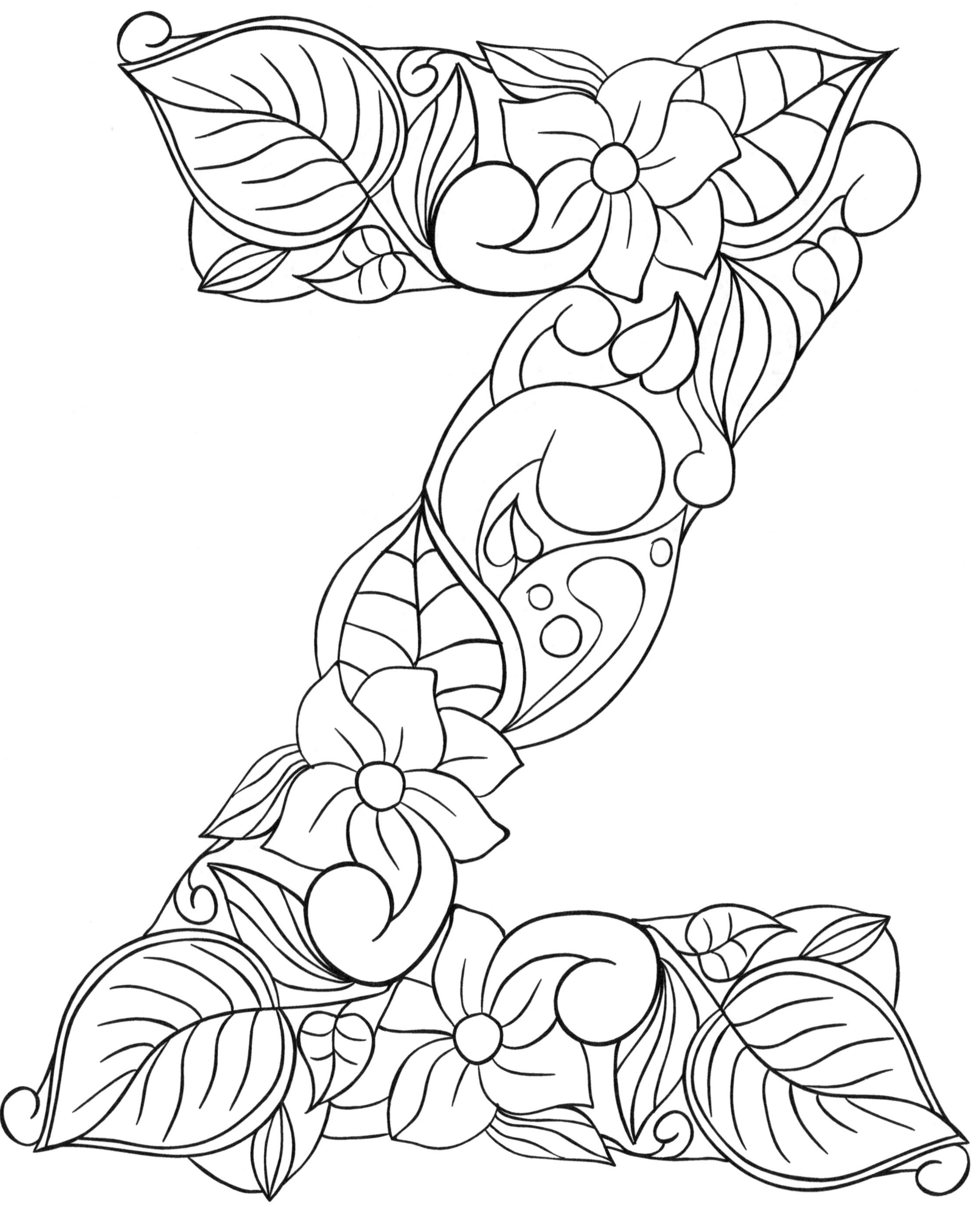

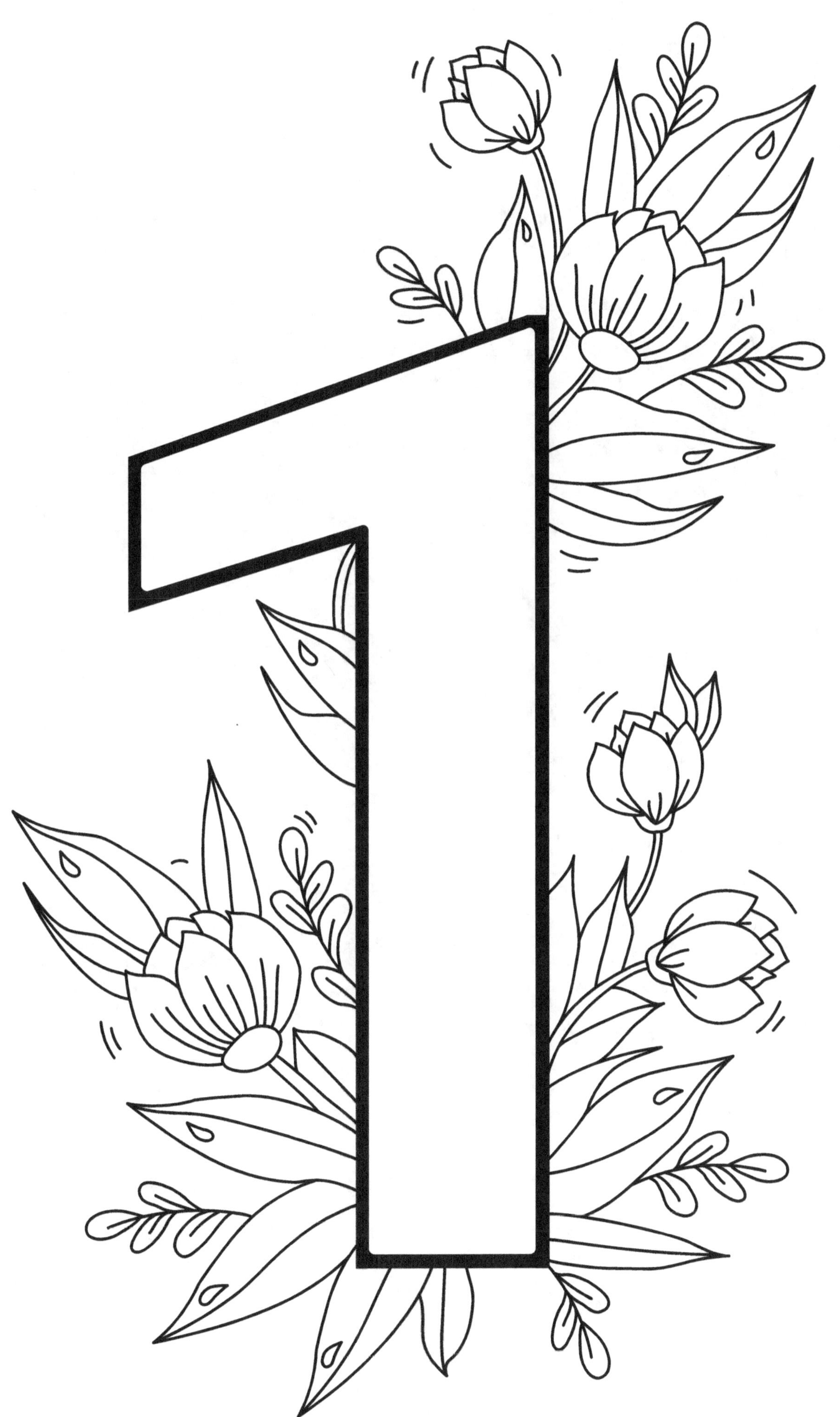

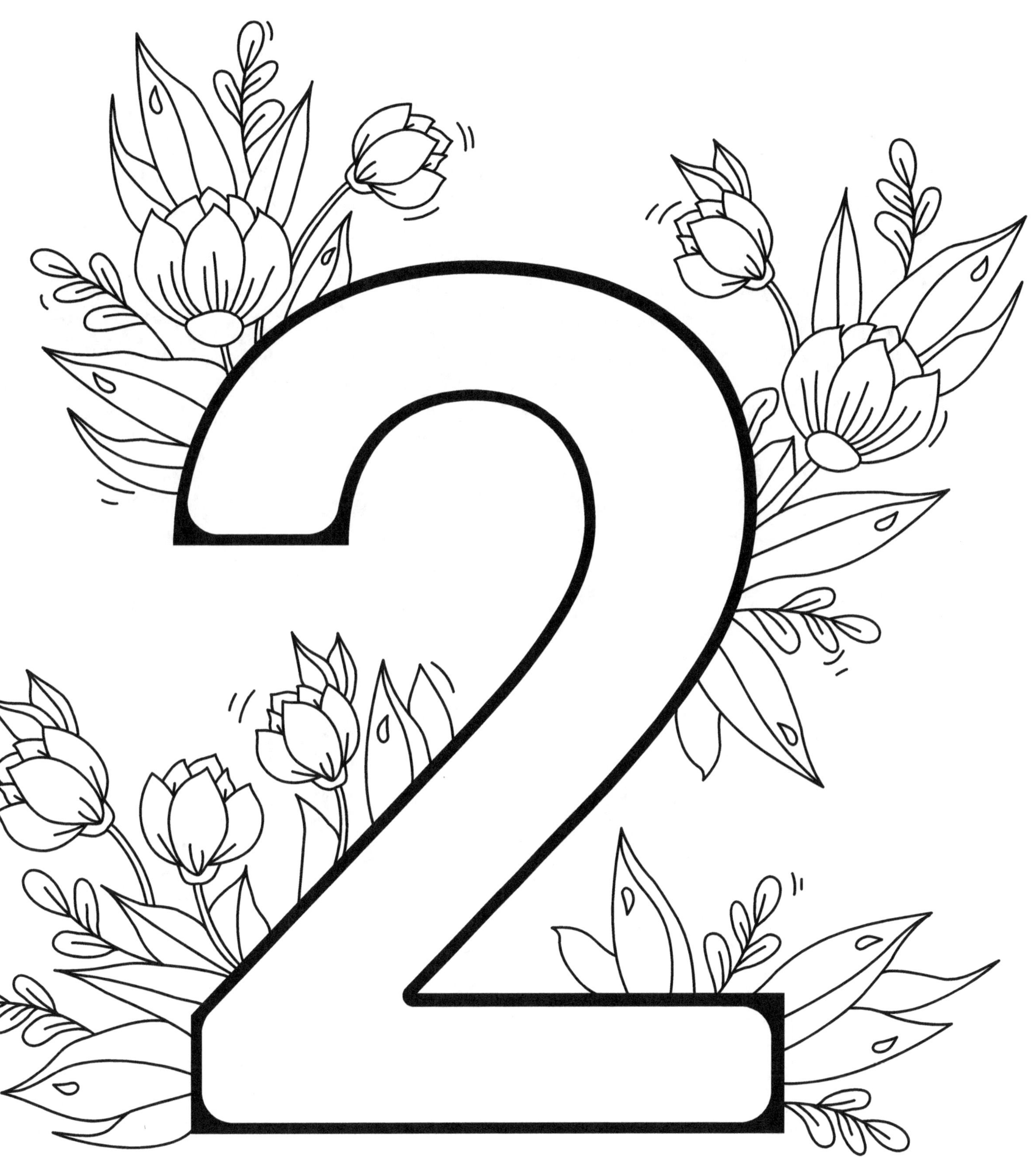

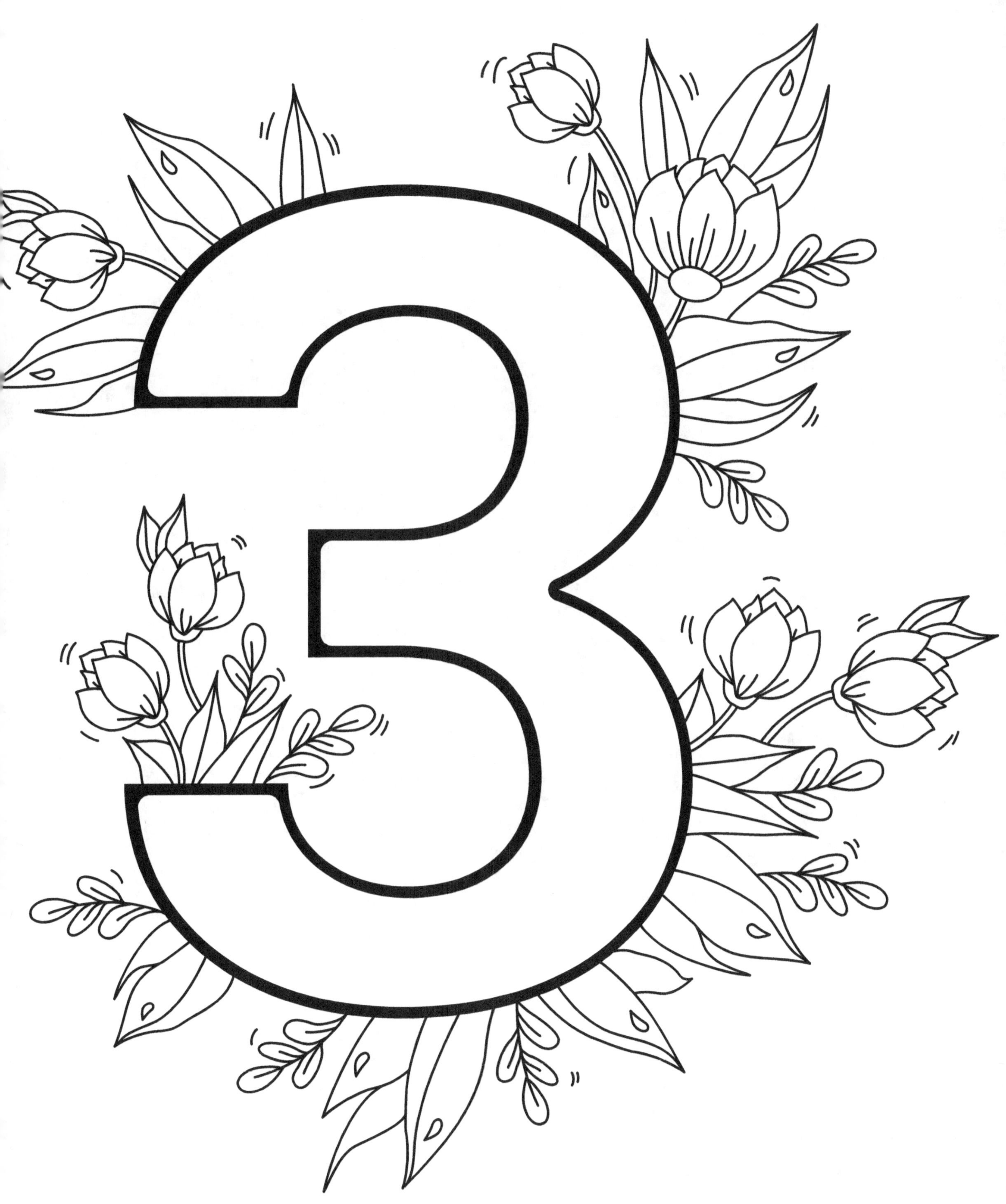

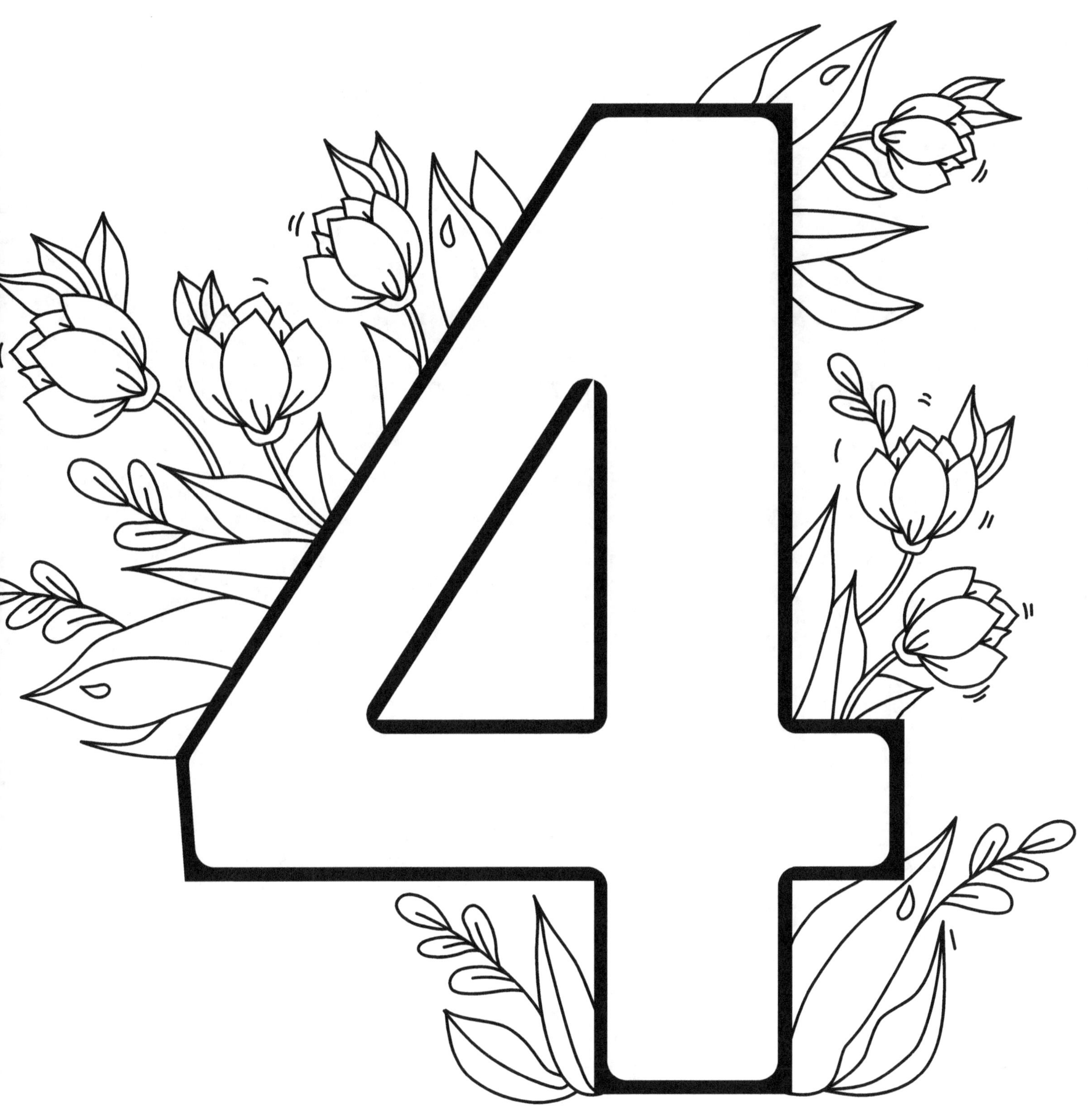

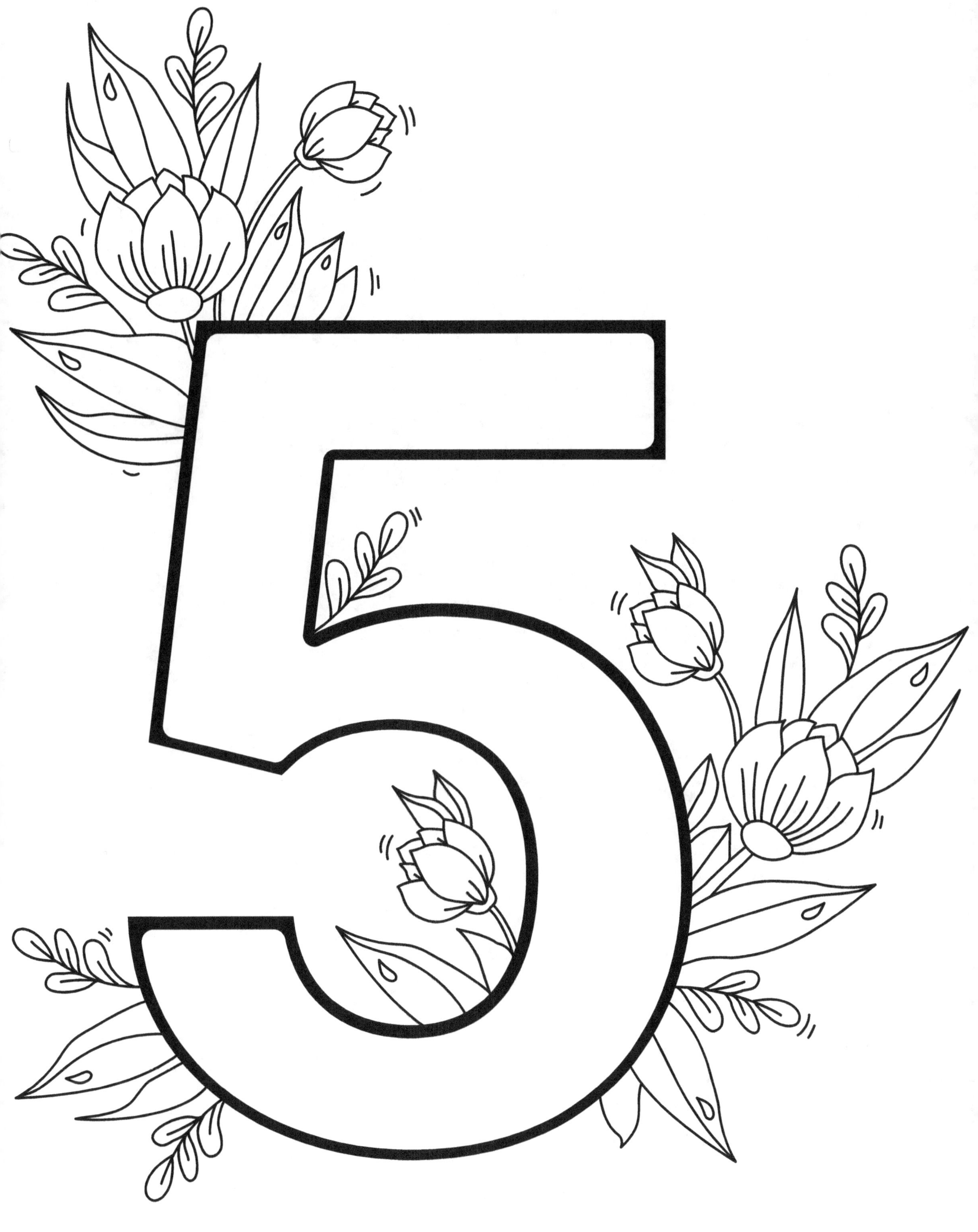

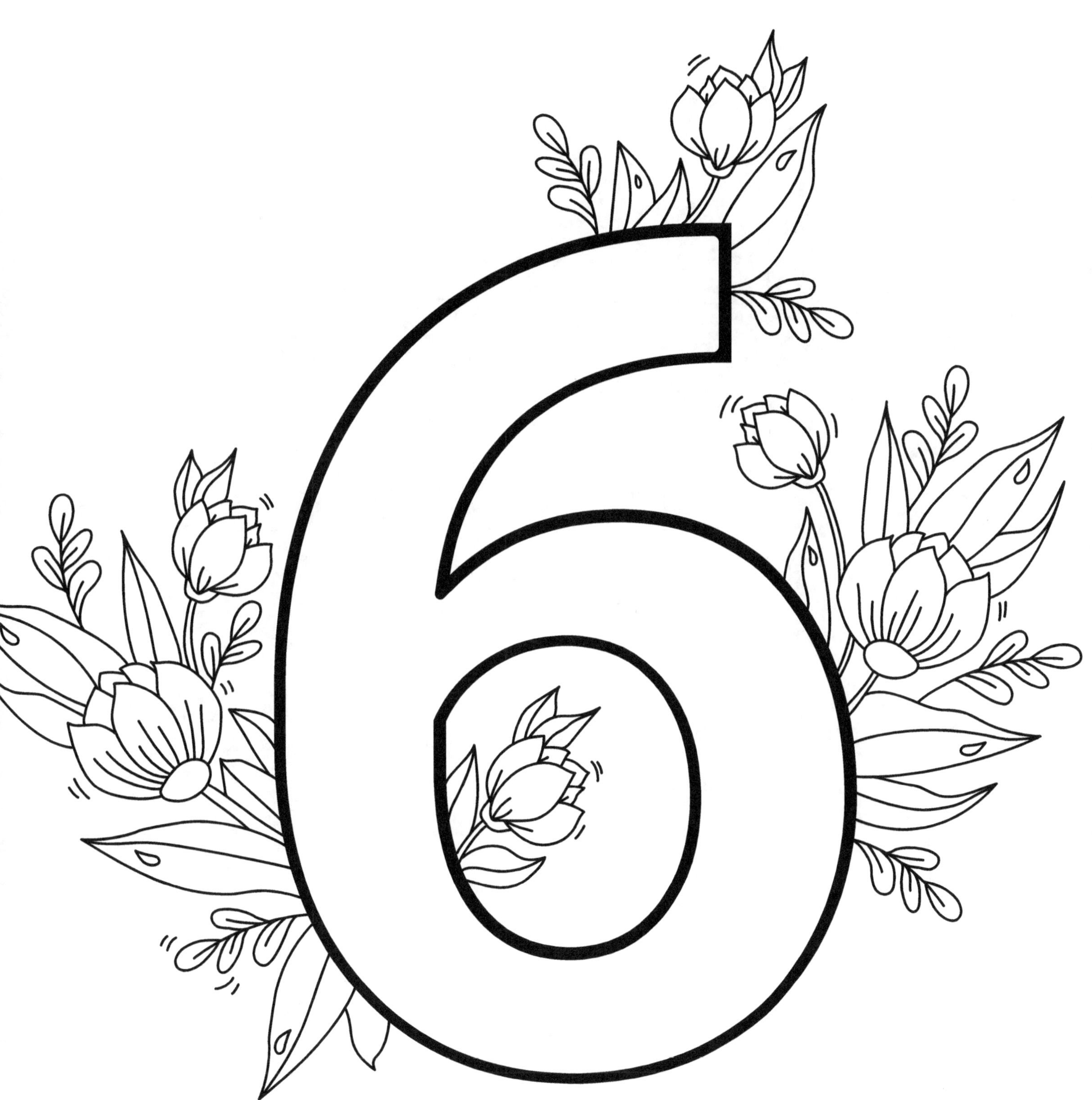

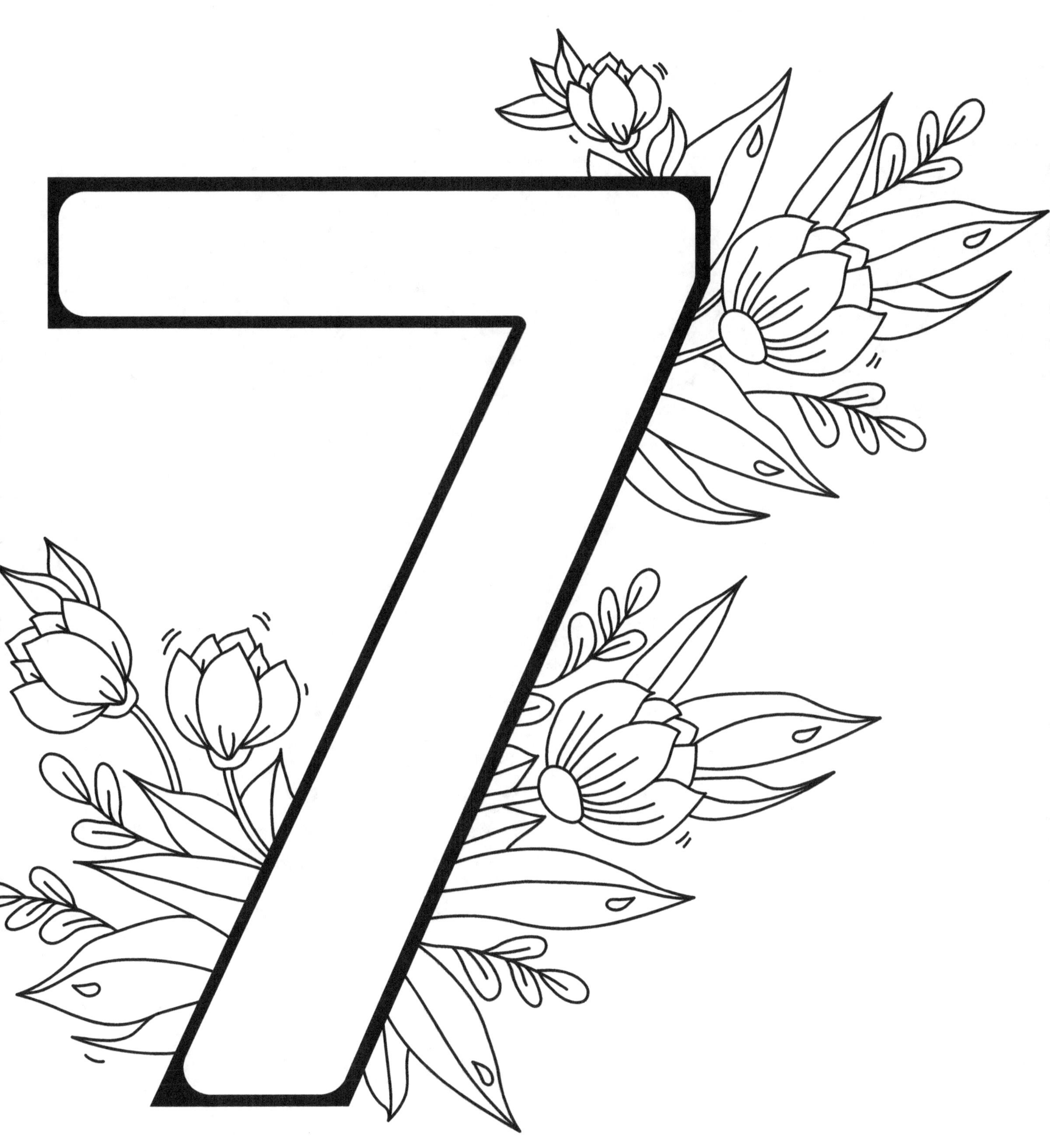

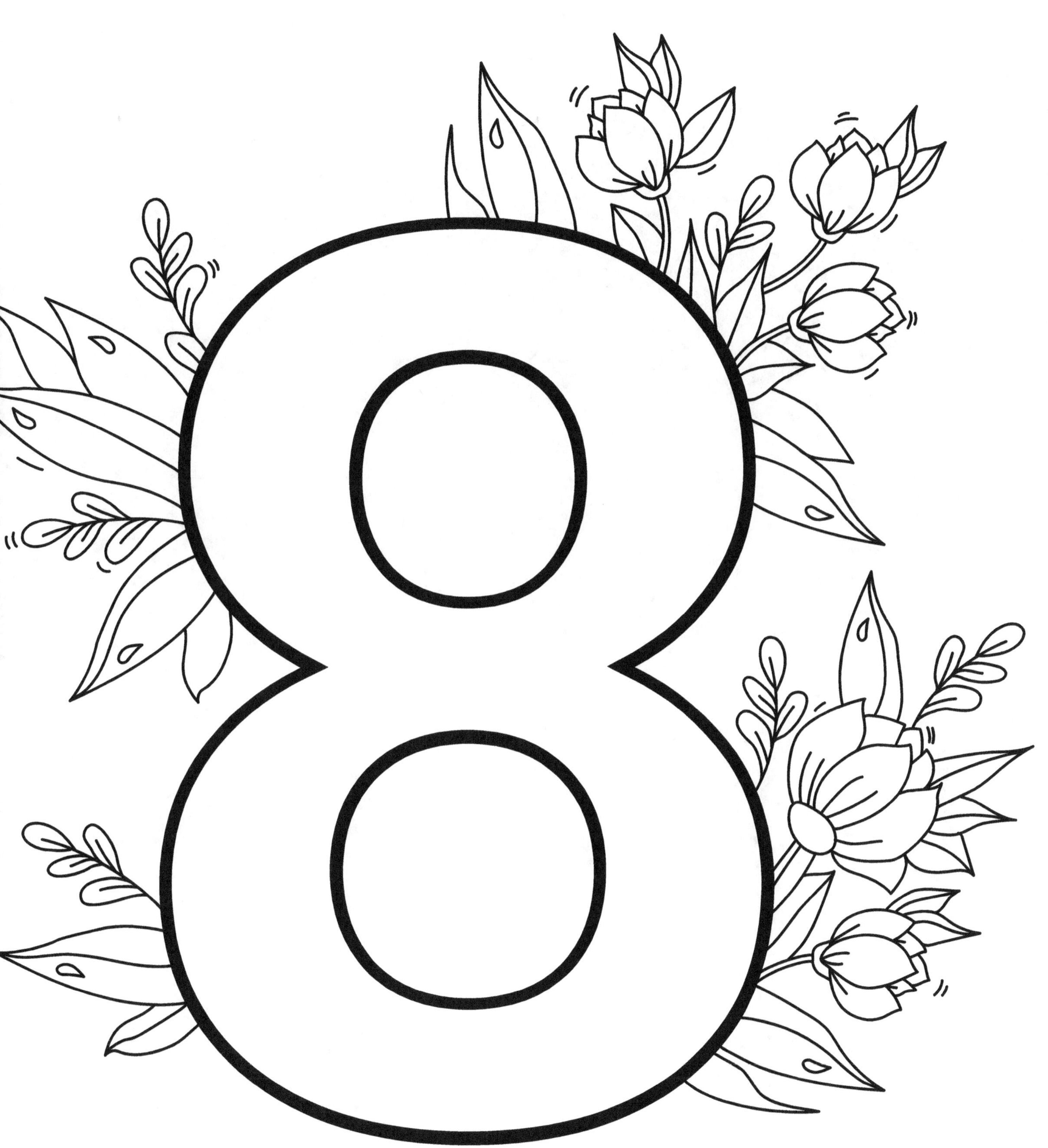

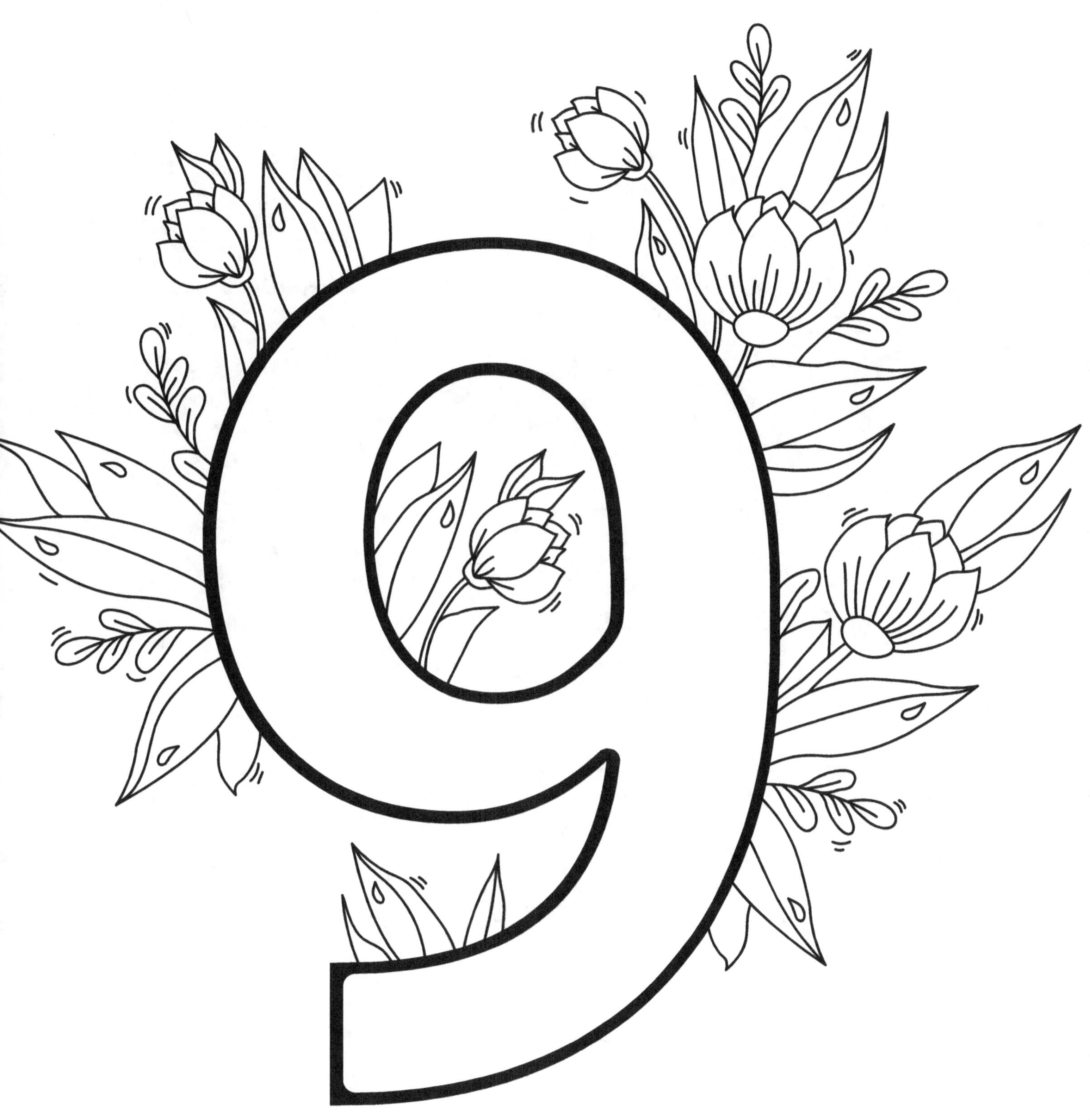

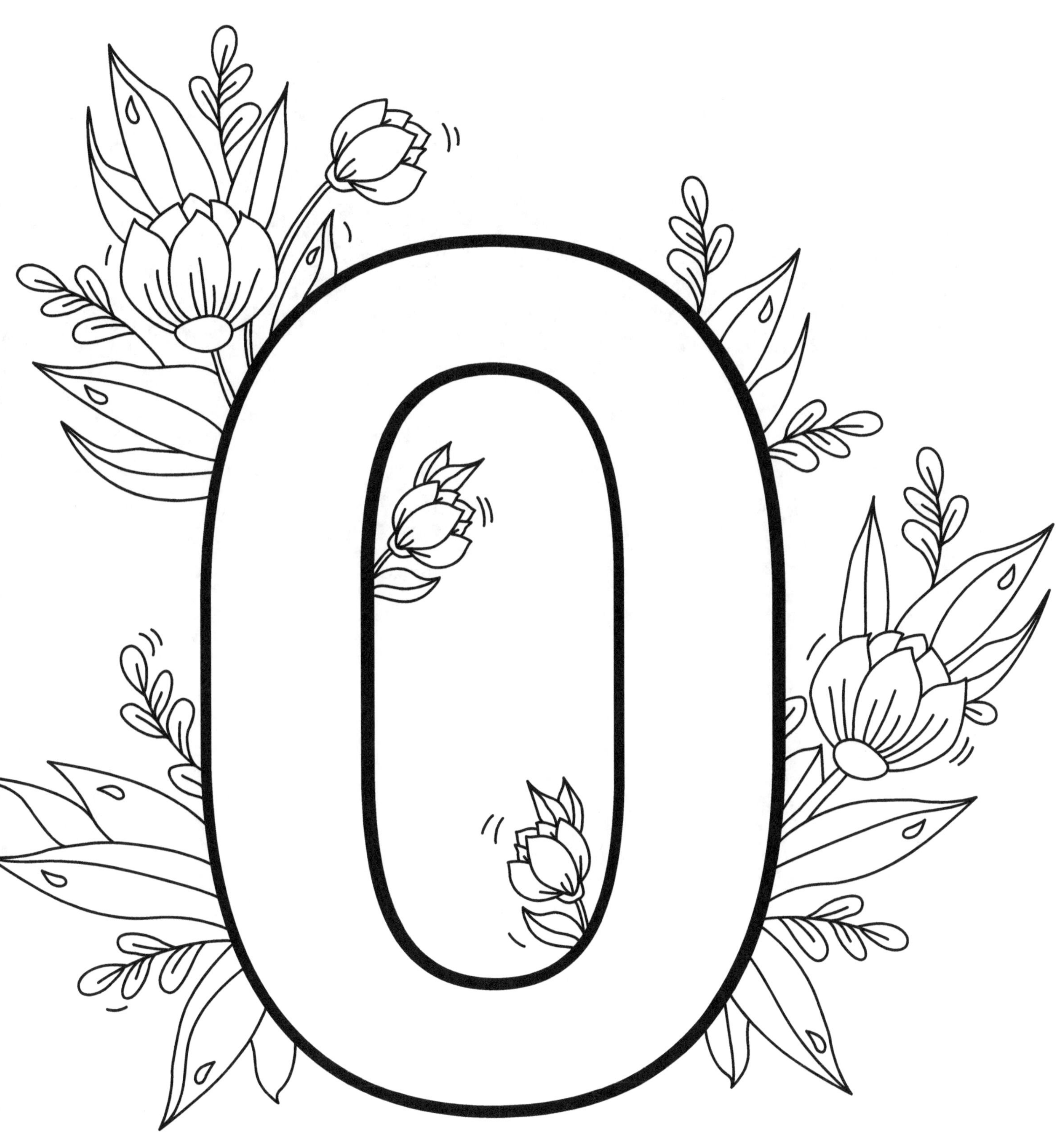

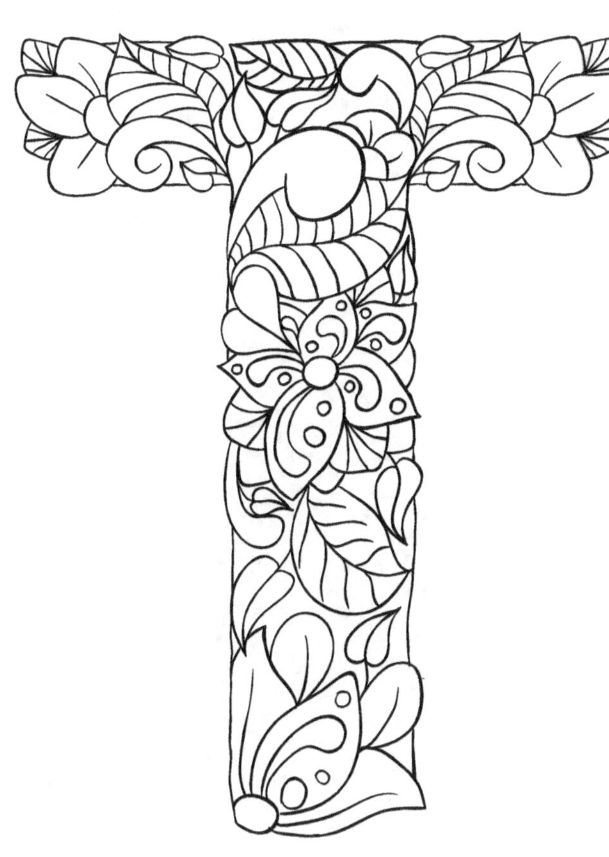

Thank

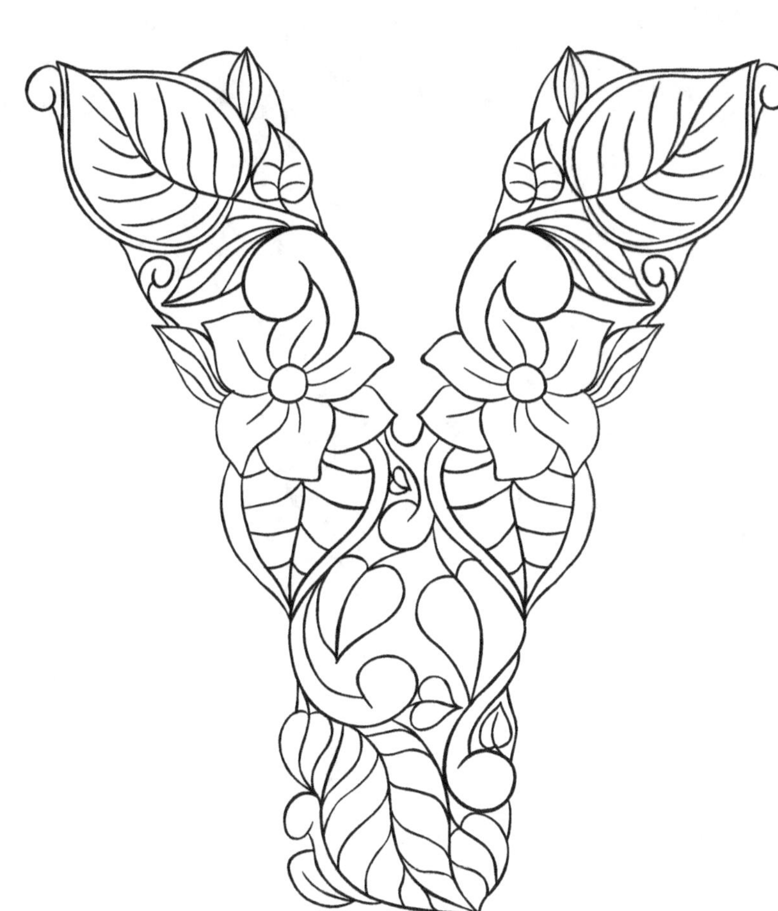

ou

Ladyhawke

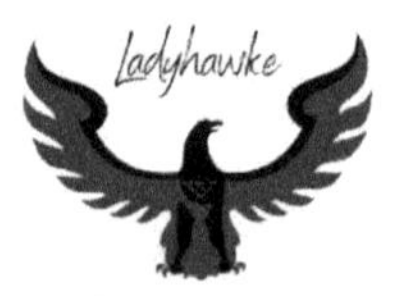